THE GOOD FIGHT OF FAITH

FOLLOWING THE EXAMPLE OF JESUS

ALAN VINCENT

DESTINY IMAGE® PUBLISHERS, INC.
P.O. Box 310, Shippensburg, PA 17257–0310

"Speaking to the Purposes of God for this Generation and for the Generations to Come."

This book and all other Destiny Image, Revival Press, Mercy Place, Fresh Bread, Destiny Image Fiction, and Treasure House books are available at Christian bookstores and distributors worldwide.

For a U.S. bookstore nearest you, call 1-800-722-6774.
For more information on foreign distributors, call 717-532-3040.
Reach us on the Internet: www.destinyimage.com.

ISBN 10: 0-7684-2652-9
ISBN 13: 978-0-7684-2652-6

For Worldwide Distribution, Printed in the U.S.A.

1 2 3 4 5 6 7 8 9 10 11 / 12 11 10 09 08

DEDICATION

I dedicate this book first to Eileen, my beloved wife and fellow warrior in the faith. Then, to our three grown children, Rachel, Duncan, and David, and our seven grandchildren, Nicola, David, Katie, Emily, Zachary, Eleanor, and Benedict—that they may become increasingly mighty in faith.

Also I dedicate this book to a purpose: to see the power of faith transform the Church so that it does the works of Jesus.

ACKNOWLEDGMENTS

As I come to thank the people who have been instrumental in seeing this book finally get into print, my mind runs through dozens of names. It is impossible to mention them all individually, but my sincere thanks go to all who were unrelenting in their insistence that I should write.

Eileen, my wife, has been a persistent encourager, knowing that what I taught had to be written. Natalie Hardy not only encouraged but offered her wisdom and practical help. Franz Lippi, Duncan Watkinson, Steve Telzerow, Larry Krieder, and reputable prophets including Hank Kunneman have all had their part in bringing this book into being. Julie Larson read and reread the manuscript as she did the editing. I thank God and recognize that I am indebted to all of you for your loving words that have kept me on target so that today we hold this book in our hands.

ENDORSEMENTS

Being a warrior, I always look for something that will increase my shield of faith. When I read *The Good Fight of Faith,* I realized this was the perfect book for the season ahead. Alan Vincent, with all the wisdom within him that the Lord has seasoned, has penned a masterpiece. My favorite chapter for all of us during this next season is "Faith for Compensation and Restitution." This book will do nothing but "build you up" and strengthen you to be a warrior whose faith shield quenches all the fiery darts of the enemy in the days ahead.

Dr. Chuck Pierce
Glory of Zion
Denton, Texas

For years I have watched my father write this journey of faith with his life in many nations, and now you can share this practical but deep biblical knowledge too. It will change your priorities, influence the way you think, and make you dangerous. *The Good Fight of Faith* is a book that will enable you to live life on the edge, experiencing a new level of financial freedom, health in your body, and satisfaction in your spirit.

Rachel Hickson,
Heartcry Ministries, UK
Author of *Supernatural Communication*
and *Little Keys Open Big Doors*

Alan Vincent is a true apostle whose amazing revelation of Scripture takes sound doctrine to an exceptional level. He gives deep meat from the Word, but in such a way that you can easily apply it. His teaching on faith is a home-run message, like none ever heard!

Hank Kunneman, Senior Pastor
Lord of Hosts Church
Omaha, Nebraska

I have heard and read much on the topic of faith, but this book is unique! As Alan shares from the Scriptures and his own experience, you will find something exploding deep within you, giving rise to a new kind of warring, overcoming faith. In our day, God desires an army of those who will step into the eternal realm and live by supernatural faith right here on the earth. This book will introduce you to that dimension of faith.

Barry Wissler
Senior Pastor, Ephrata Community Church
Founder, HarvestNET
Ephrata, Pennsylvania

What a great book! *The Good Fight of Faith* should be read by every pastor and every believer in Christ. This biblically sound book on faith is filled with practical application. The stories from Alan's life of faith are tremendous. Faith continued to build in my life as I read through each chapter. I highly recommend this book. You will never be the same!

Larry Krieder
Senior Pastor
D.O.V.E International

Of the books I have read, this one contains the greatest revelation regarding faith. My life has been transformed as a result of obeying and applying these principles. Many of the revelations that I know today I owe to apostle Alan Vincent, who has been like a father to me. If you read and obey the message in this book, your life also will be changed.

Guillermo Maldonado
Pastor, El Rey Jesús
Miami, Florida

Alan Vincent has personally practiced the principles written in this book. The in-depth teaching in this book will undo many wrong notions and radically amend the mindset of people concerning practical Christian faith and challenge them to be overcomers. This book is a precious gift to those who are earnestly seeking to exercise higher levels of faith and will leave a long-lasting impact in the lives of its readers.

Rev. Y. Mohan Babu
Senior Pastor, Sion Fellowship
Hyderabad, India

For over 30 years, I have known Alan as a man of faith who has always inspired me to trust and obey our Lord. This book captures the essence of his life and teaching. It not only informs the mind, but it also impacts the spirit and imparts true faith. Our unbelieving generation needs this book desperately, and I hope it will be read and reread until God raises up many mighty men and women of faith.

Duncan Watkinson
Founder, India Revival Network
Bangalore, India

We live in a world of global challenges and uncertainties. It seems that the faith of many has been shaken, causing disillusionments, disappointments, and discouragements. Thus, their vision of hope and faith is blurred, distracting them from God's intended destiny for their lives. Alan Vincent's book is a timely and critical message that reminds us of the proper foundations and order of faith, as well as equips us to fight the good fight of faith, according to the spirit, not the flesh. Alan is uniquely qualified as a senior statesmen and ambassador to remind us of who we are in Christ and who Christ is in us. He does not speak as a theorist, but as one who, through the crucibles of experience, leads us with great expectation to the purposes of God. I found myself filled with a renewed hunger for God's will in my life and ministry. The need for courageous and persevering leadership is needed more today than ever before. I believe this book will be used as a much-needed source of equipping and encouragement to stay the course and fight the good fight of faith. Thank you, Alan, for sharing your life journey and kingdom nuggets that will empower us all. Paul, the apostle, said to follow him as he followed Christ. Alan, because of your life of integrity and consistency, many can confidently follow you as you follow Christ.

Dr. Doug Stringer
Founder, Somebody Cares International
Houston, Texas

Alan Vincent has blessed us with tremendous truth. The truth that makes all things possible for those who know how to appreciate and exercise the faith of God. Alan does not share these life-giving truths just from book learning but from many decades of demonstrating the workability of the truths he presents. Without faith it is impossible for us to be and do what God has called us to be and do. The principles presented will enable readers to do the works of Christ and fulfill their destiny.

Dr. Bill Hamon
Bishop of Christian International Ministries Network (CIMN)
Author of *Day of the Saints,* and others

CONTENTS

PREFACE

Faith is one of those words that Christians use frequently but with very little understanding of what it really means.

To some it is primarily a means of becoming wealthy through obeying the biblical principles of generous giving. We tap into these great spiritual laws of the Kingdom and find them working for us. "Kingdom Stock" is proclaimed as the best possible investment which in the long run will outdo "Wall Street" every time. But these spiritual laws also teach us that the right, biblical balance is to live in modest sufficiency ourselves while releasing "abundance for every good work" of God through grace and faith (see 2 Cor. 9:8).

To powerfully advance the Kingdom some great financial breakthroughs are necessary, and they do miraculously occur through real faith. But the focus should not be on ourselves and our needs, but on the resources needed to forcefully advance the Kingdom of God. Jesus promised that if we seek His Kingdom first then all our material necessities will be automatically supplied as well (see Matt. 6:33).

For others, faith is something we may need occasionally, but only in an emergency. It is a bit like the spare wheel in the trunk of our car. We know it is there but hope we never have to use it, and, just like having to change a wheel, we are not even sure how to do it should the emergency occur. Should such a crisis happen, we quickly turn to some other expert for help and never develop any real faith of our own.

In America, for the average Christian, faith is not part of our daily life, for there are always several alternatives. It's possible to live for months without ever needing to exercise any real faith because we rely instead on credit cards, a good medical service, plus many other forms of insurance, so that we are rarely cast upon God in naked desperation.

Faith is rarely seen as our mightiest spiritual weapon against the devil which, when fully understood, properly developed, and skillfully used, is capable of giving us many great victories over the evil one and all his forces.

This book is devoted primarily to that purpose.

INTRODUCTION

B
Y A.D. 68-69, the apostle Paul had seen God move in tremendous ways. Whole cities had been shaken by the power of God. Mighty miracles had occurred. Men had been raised from the dead at his hands. Young men like Timothy, Titus, and Epaphroditus had been saved out of pagan darkness and become wonderful apostles.

However, Paul had also experienced some terrible times when the Lord seemed to abandon him. Outside the city of Lystra, he was stoned and left for dead (see Acts 14:19-20). Where was God then? After a promising start as a gifted evangelist, Alexander the coppersmith refused Paul's correction, turned against him, and was now doing Paul much harm (see 1 Tim. 1:18-20; 2 Tim. 4:14).

In Second Corinthians 11:24-33, Paul lists some of the trials of his faith. He had been beaten five times with a whip and three times with a rod. He had been left shipwrecked. He had gone without food. Most painful of all, the churches in Asia had forsaken him. He had experienced the anguish of covenant brothers walking out on him, and they were now opposing him. The apostle Paul had seen some churches wonderfully established and others ravished by the devil and ripped to pieces (see 2 Cor. 11:24-29).

If anyone had been through hardships, this man had. By A.D. 68-69, he had seen almost everything and could look back over more than thirty years of ministry. It was at this point that he wrote these crucial instructions to Timothy, his true son in the faith. Paul had been in prison for several years and was probably writing from prison or during a brief release.

He was certainly not teaching theory from an air-conditioned studio or a luxurious apartment. Like a relay runner, he was finishing his lap and was handing the baton over to Timothy who was to run the next lap. He was giving commandments that would undergird Timothy's life and impact many generations to come.

Paul gave certain commandments to Timothy. They are recorded in First Timothy 6:12-14 as follows:

- "Fight the good fight of faith" (1 Tim. 6:12).

- "Lay hold on the eternal life, to which you were also called" (1 Tim. 6:12).

- Maintain the good confession which you have confessed in the presence of many witnesses (see 1 Tim. 6:12).

The first commandment, which Paul told Timothy to keep blamelessly, was to *fight the good fight of faith* (1 Tim. 6:12). This instruction was not a matter of choice, nor did it depend on how he felt or whether it was convenient. It was a command!

When writing his second farewell letter to Timothy, Paul knew that his time had come, and he was about to be executed. He made that very clear in Second Timothy 4:6: "I am already being poured out as a drink offering, and the time of my departure is at hand" (2 Tim. 4:6). In the next verse he summarized his 30-plus years of service to the Lord: "I have fought the good fight, I have finished the race, I have kept the faith" (2 Tim. 4:7). His ministry had been one long fight from beginning to end.

This command to "fight the good fight of faith" continues for all of us to this present day (1 Tim. 6:12).

The only alternative to fighting a good fight of faith is to come to terms of peace with the devil and settle down to some compromised passivity. In reality, like Paul, we have no alternative but to fight.

CHAPTER 1

THE GOOD FIGHT OF FAITH

The Bible calls our life a race of faith (see Heb. 12:1-2). In racing terms, it is a marathon, not a 100 meter sprint. In fighting terms, it is a fifteen-round contest and not a three-round bout. You've got to last to the end! In First Timothy 6:12, the Greek word for "fight" is *agonizomai*. Our English words "agonize" and "agony" come from this root. It literally means "to struggle with perseverance."

We must aim to win the race and complete the course. Our Christian life is not a walk in the park but one long battle of faith. That's why Paul told Timothy, *Well, son, it was one long good fight for me. All I'm promising you, as I hand you the baton of apostolic ministry, is that you will have to continue to fight that long good fight of faith.*

IT'S A GOOD FIGHT

Paul used one adjective to describe this fight. He did not simply write, "I have fought a fight of faith," but said, "I have fought the good fight" (2 Tim. 4:7). What is a *good* fight? It is one that we win! Here the *good fight* is "the fight"—it extends the Kingdom of God and brings His glory. It is the fight that God initiates. It is the fight ordained for us.

TIME, ETERNITY, AND FAITH

Hebrews 11:6 says that without faith it is impossible to please God and that those who come to God must do two things: 1) They must believe that God is, and 2) They must believe that He rewards those who diligently seek Him.

GOD IS

First, they must believe that God is. Before moving into the Bible's definition of faith, I want to lay some foundation on what this phrase means. God is not a "was," a "now," or a "is-going-to-be" God. He just *is*.

In order to move in faith, you must understand that there is an eternal realm outside the limits of this time-space world in which we live. When we move into the eternal realm, we move out of time into a new dimension completely. There are at least four, and possibly more, dimensions by which we measure this created physical world. We have length, breadth, height, and time.

Maybe the following diagram will help us to begin to understand this mystery.

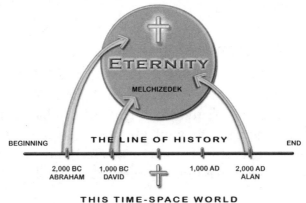

Think of time as a line. There was a moment when time began, and it has continued chronologically ever since. We are told there will come another moment when time as we have known it will come to an end. Until then, our natural lives in this time-space world are largely governed and measured by time. However, time is relative and not absolute.

Physicists, probing even more deeply into the mysteries of creation, report that they are now able to demonstrate that when a sub-atomic particle of matter is accelerated to near the speed of light, time slows down. Time continues to slow down until it reaches the speed of light, at which point time actually stands still. Eternity could possibly be a state of living at the energy level of the speed of light.

Imagine that some time in the future a group of astronauts leaves the Earth in a space capsule that can accelerate to a speed of over 170,000 miles per second as they go on a visit to a distant planet several light years away. Traveling at that speed, they would be traveling close to the speed of light, which is about 186,000 miles per second. Imagine they finally returned to Earth after being away for 20 years. We would be amazed when they stepped out of the spaceship because they would look exactly the same as when they left. From our perspective, 20 years would have passed, but from their perspective only about four hours would have elapsed. The difference between these two time perspectives would be due to the different energy levels at which we had been living.

The eternal realm does not just consist of time as we know it endlessly going by. It is better thought of as a timeless, eternal now. If we imagine time as we know it as a line stretching from the beginning to the end of time, we could call this line "history." There are many events that have already taken place, and some events that will take place in the future at different points on that time line.

However, when it comes to eternity, it is better to think of it like a circle. It has no beginning, and it has no end. When you step into eternity, you step into all of it at once. Everything just is, and you can touch all of it simultaneously at the same moment.

In some of our traditional hymns, we sing about eternity in terms of endless time. One great hymn has these lines: "When we've been there ten thousand years, bright shining as the sun, we've no less days to sing God's praise than when we first begun." In truth, eternity is not a long time. It is not time at all but one glorious, continuous now. The natural habitat for God is this eternal realm, but He is also able to enter and move about in time wherever and whenever He chooses. Time is something God has created to go with this time-space physical world. Faith operates in the eternal realm, and to move in faith you have to be able to step out from the time-line of events taking place historically into the eternal realm, where all that God has spoken into existence is simultaneously available to be grasped hold of by faith.

There are many events that are of great importance in the spiritual realm that did happen at particular points of time, and it is important to recognize that they are truly historical. However, as they happened in time, they simultaneously became eternal and also filled all of eternity with their power.

The greatest example is the cross on which Jesus died. In First Peter 1:20 we are told Jesus was that precious Lamb without spot whose sacrifice was "foreordained before the foundation of the world" (1 Pet. 1:20). Yet we know that Jesus was crucified at a particular point in history. In time, that was about 2000 years ago, but that event was not only an event in time, it was also an event in eternity. It not only touched the temporary realm of time, but it also invaded the eternal realm of the spirit and became a powerful "now" event stretching from the beginning to the end of time. As Jesus was being physically crucified in time, He spiritually stepped into eternity, and the power of that cross gloriously filled all eternity. Although there was a point in time when it happened, it became an eternal now as far as its efficacy is concerned. Therefore, the ever-fresh, powerful shedding of His blood never gets old because it is an eternal thing that never needs to be repeated. He is constantly the freshly slain Lamb of God (see Heb. 10:18-23).

In John 8:56-58, Jesus told the Pharisees and scribes, "Abraham rejoiced to see my day." They replied, "You are not yet 50 years old, how can you have seen Abraham?" Jesus replied, "Before Abraham was I am." (See John 8:56-58.)

In John 11:25-27, Jesus declared, "I [already] am the resurrection and the life," and then asked Martha, "Do you believe this?" She replied, "Yes, Lord." (See John 11:25-27.)

Abraham, in his spirit man, stepped into eternity two thousand years before Jesus was crucified in time. As he stepped into eternity, he entered the eternal realm where the cross already is. He embraced the power of that cross, was cleansed by the blood of Jesus, and had fellowship with Jesus in the person of Melchizedek, the high priest of the New Covenant, who gave him bread and wine. From that moment, he enjoyed an unveiled New Covenant relationship with God. As Abraham fellowshipped with Melchizedek, he met God face to face and became His friend. There was no need for any animal to be sacrificed, because the perfect Lamb had already done His perfect work. He did not have to fulfill any rules and regulations of the Mosaic law. Instead, Abraham lived in all the glory of the New Covenant two thousand years before it was initiated in time. In his spirit man, he stepped from this time world into eternity, and he began to live in all the benefits of what Jesus did on the cross as a present, eternal reality.

David must have had an amazing vision in which he seemed to be actually watching the crucifixion of Jesus as a present reality. He recorded it for us all in Psalm 22. As a result, He created a new tabernacle, called David's tabernacle, without curtains or divisions and where nothing of the Mosaic law was practiced. Here, David and others lived continually in the unveiled presence of God. At that same point in time, there were many meticulous Mosaic law keepers frequenting Moses' tabernacle trying to be justified by works. It is likely that if they had tried to enter the tabernacle of David on the basis of their works, they would have dropped dead instantly.

However, because David was living according to the New Covenant and only trusting in the power of the freshly slain blood of the Lamb to make him righteous, he, along with other believers, could behold the very glory of the Lord without coming to any harm. David with unveiled face could just stand in God's presence, love Him with all his heart, and permanently live just to obey Him. Regardless of the fact that David was not of the tribe of Levi, he lived as a priest in unveiled intimacy with God one thousand years before the veil sealing off the Holiest of All was ripped open from top to bottom. David could do that because when the veil was ripped on Earth at the same moment in time that Jesus died, it also immediately became an eternal event.

Each one of us can either live in time as a natural man or woman, or we can live in spirit in the eternal realm like our great forefathers Abraham and David. It is possible to live in the power and benefits of the eternal realm while still here on Earth. If you start to do that, you can move in faith and make things happen that are impossible by any other means.

Second Corinthians 4:18 says that the things which are seen are temporary, but the things which are not seen are eternal. You have to get yourself delivered from your rational—*I've got to touch it, feel it, see it, and have it explained to me before I can believe it*— thinking. Faith has none of these limitations. You don't need to understand it. You don't need to see it. You don't need to hear it or feel it naturally. You just need to know that it already is. You can grab hold of it by your spirit, and then it becomes an activity of faith that is incredibly powerful.

All of this comes out of this one little phrase: "You have to believe that God is" (see Heb. 11:6). You have to believe that God is eternal. It is not simply saying that you have to believe that God exists; even the devil believes that. You have to believe in the eternal now that God is.

GOD IS A REWARDER

Second, you have to believe that He rewards those who diligently seek Him (see Heb. 11:6). You cannot seek God and waste your time. You cannot seek God and suffer loss. There is nothing more rewarding, rich, and beneficial in every way than seeking God. What you get out of it is immeasurable in its value. Not only does it bless you, but you then become a river of blessing to other people.

BIBLE DEFINITION OF FAITH

Many Christians use the term *faith* without understanding what it really means. Before I continue, I must warn you about three close relatives of faith, which are hope, knowledge, and presumption.

The first relative of faith is hope. This is often a good thing and may be a step on the way to real faith, but it is not the same as faith and must not be confused with real faith. Hope still carries an attitude of uncertainty that real faith never has.

The second relative is knowledge. I'm using the word "knowledge" in the sense that a person will only "believe" when he or she perceives something has already happened with his or her natural senses. If you wait to see, hear, feel, or know something naturally before you can believe, then you are moving in knowledge and not faith. If you wait for this knowledge to come before you will believe, then it is too late for faith.

The third relative is presumption. Presumption is attempting to claim by faith something that you want, rather than grabbing something that God has clearly already spoken into existence in the eternal realm. It does not yet exist in the eternal realm, and you are trying to create or force it into existence by your "faith."

These three close relatives are not actually faith, but they are often confused with faith. We will look at each of them more closely, but first let's look at what the Bible says that faith is.

Hebrews 11:1 provides the Bible's definition of faith:

Now faith is the substance of things hoped for, the evidence of things not seen (Hebrews 11:1).

This definition begins with a simple declaration, "Now faith is..." Faith can never be spoken of in the future tense. It is always in the present tense. It functions in the present tense, but it is based upon something that has already happened and was completed in the past.

There are several places in Scripture, although it is not so obvious in most English translations, where the original Greek text puts two tenses together when speaking about faith. They are the future and the past perfect tenses. It is strange grammatically, but it makes perfect sense spiritually. For example, in Mark's Gospel, Jesus says,

Therefore I say to you, whatever things you ask when you pray, believe that you [have already] *receive*[d] *them [past perfect tense], and you will have them* [future tense] (Mark 11:24).

The past perfect tense and the future tense are joined together. Essentially the verse says that before you can have something in the future, you must have already possessed it by faith as a past event in the spirit realm. Another example of this construction is found in Matthew 16:19 and again in Matthew 18:18 where Jesus says "whatever you bind on earth..." or "whatever you loose on earth..." (Matt. 18:18).

He uses the same past and future tense put together. Literally it says, *whatever you bind on earth will be, because it already has been bound in Heaven.*

Before you can see something happen on Earth as a result of binding or loosing, you have to know that it has already been done in the heavenlies. You will never see it manifested on Earth until you know it is a "has been" in the realm of the spirit.

You have to be certain of the "now" of something in order to materially possess it by faith in the future. I have to be able to say, "I know I am healed." That is the "now" tense. You know you are healed because you know that it has already been done in the heavenly realm, even though you may still be waiting for the physical manifestation on Earth.

The language of faith is in the "now" because it is based on the certainty of what has already taken place. It cannot be in the future tense because faith cannot exist without already having laid hold of something. Faith has absolute confidence that in the near future there will be the physical manifestation of what faith has already laid hold of. This means that you can speak confidently now concerning the future.

FAITH IS SUBSTANCE (ASSURANCE)

Hebrews 11:1 uses two important words that are essential to understanding faith. Both words were used in the legal profession.

The first phrase says that "faith is the substance..." (Heb. 11:1). This word *substance* is also translated "assurance" or "confidence." The Greek word is *hupostasis* and literally means "to be under the authority of." When the Bible was being written, this word was widely used in the legal profession. It was used to describe a package of legal documents that gave a person undisputed title to a piece of land or property. We would call it the "title deed."

It was a written document describing the boundaries of the land or property that a person owned. With that legal document, you were the undisputed owner of that property. Every dispute about the land came under the authority of what that document said. It was yours because you had the title deed. Therefore, we can say that faith is the "title deed" of things hoped for.

When buying a house, once you have made an offer, you pass through a nail-biting period while the legal matters are settled. When someone asks, "Do you have a new house?" You probably would say, "I hope so," while the legalities are being completed. Until those legal documents are signed, sealed, and delivered, you do not have the absolute, settled assurance that you have it. Once you have the completed title deed, you can say with authority, "Yes, I have my new house!"

Imagine that a CEO of a large group of chain stores is living in London. He decides to put up a store in San Antonio, Texas. He does not have time to visit the city personally, so he hires a local agent to find a suitable site and make all the arrangements. The CEO has drawings, schematics, and illustrations of the store he is going to build. He can picture the building perfectly and is already imagining the profit he is going to make.

At this stage, the CEO is in the phase of *hope*. If you were to ask him if he was going to build that new store, he would answer, "Well, I sure hope so." However, nothing is actually happening yet because he is waiting for something. He's waiting for the legal formalities to be completed that give him undisputed title to the land and permission to build.

Then one day he receives a package containing all the necessary legal documents. The arrival of the title deed changes everything. As soon as he has those documents in his hand, he moves from hope to faith. Immediately, he calls the bank to release the money and instructs the architects and the construction company to get on site and start building. He didn't need to go to the site physically. He never saw anything with his eyes, but the moment he read the words of the title deed, he knew he was on solid ground to move forward.

Before that moment, he only had a dream. The title deed provided full assurance that he owned the land, had the legal right to build on it, and could legally bring forth the physical manifestation of what he had been hoping for. Faith is the title deed of things hoped for. It takes you from dreams, longings, and hopes to the place where you know you have the legal right and ownership of the thing that you are reaching out for in the realm of the spirit.

FAITH IS EVIDENCE (CONVINCING PROOF)

The second important word in Hebrews 11:1 is the Greek word *elegchos*, which means "evidence or convincing proof." This word, also a legal word, was often used in criminal courts. When a prosecuting attorney wanted to convict an alleged criminal of a crime, he would stand before the jury and present the evidence of his case and persuade them to see it his way. The attorney would present his "convincing proof" with such persuasive verbal arguments that the jury felt like they had actually been eyewitnesses to the crime.

The jury would be so convinced by the evidence that they would bring a guilty verdict against the accused without any doubt whatsoever. It was as if they had seen the crime with their own eyes. They behaved like people who had been eyewitnesses even though they had not actually been there or seen anything. Real faith from God can have this effect upon us. It persuades us to the extent that we see things as absolute reality, although we have not actually seen them with our eyes at all. God's faith brings us to exactly the same conviction and attitude that a persuaded jury has after hearing the prosecuting attorney's convincing proofs.

This is how the Bible describes faith. It has the power to bring you from dreams to substance, from hope to faith. You are able to behave just as if you have certain knowledge through your natural senses before anything is visible to them. Obviously, if jury members refuse to believe anything they have not seen with their own eyes, they will never be convinced by the evidence, and they will never convict anyone of any crime. No one in a jury has ever seen the crime actually happen. They have to rely solely on the evidence. That is what real faith is able to do.

If we refuse to believe until we can touch something with our fingers, see it with our own eyes, or feel it with our hands, then it is impossible for God to bring us to faith. If we say, "I will only believe what I can physically experience or observe with my natural senses," it is too late for faith. Once a healing has already taken place, faith is not needed.

You now have natural *knowledge* that the healing has taken place. You are an eyewitness to the healing, not someone who has been persuaded by evidence presented by God's Spirit. Faith by definition has to be able to grab hold of something before it is there in material manifestation.

A genuine, legal title deed is sufficient proof that the land is there and actually exists, even if you have never seen the land. Things for which we have faith are already there in the heavenly realm but are not yet manifested in the physical world in which we live.

FAITH CANNOT CREATE

Notice that faith is the substance of *things*, and the evidence of *things*, not dreams, not hopes, not imaginations (see Heb. 11:1). The word "things" is used twice in this simple sentence. It is talking about tangible realities. The fact that they are not yet materially existent does not mean they do not yet exist. They are unseen, but they are real nonetheless.

Many people are misled into trying to create "by faith" things that do not actually exist. Faith is not able to do that. Faith cannot create; it can only obtain. You simply cannot have a genuine, legal title deed for land that does not exist just by drawing one. That would be a forgery. Non-existent land cannot be created just by making a fictitious title deed. An attorney cannot plead a convincing case in court with invented evidence for a crime that did not take place. Trying to grab hold of something by faith that does not already exist is *presumption.*

Presumption is trying to use faith to create things that do not yet exist in the spirit realm. If something is to be obtained by faith, it may not yet be manifested in the natural world, but it must already have been spoken into existence in the spirit realm by the word of God. The Bible says the things which are seen (visible earthly things) are temporary, but the things which are not seen (spiritual things), are eternal (see 2 Cor. 4:18). The things in the spirit realm, which you cannot see naturally, are actually more real and more permanent than the things you can see in the physical world. We are not dealing with imagination, but with realities.

The only vehicle that can create things out of nothing is the word of God. God speaks things into existence out of nothing by His word. It is normal for God to create things in the realm of the spirit before they are manifested in the material realm. Once His word is there in the spirit realm, faith can get hold of what He has said and bring it into manifestation in this material, time-space world in which we live. Genuine faith gets hold of things in the spiritual realm in the same way that our hands grasp a glass of water in the natural realm.

God speaks, and out of His being comes forth this creative force that is called His Word. The Word of God is part of God. It actually is God. John 1:1 declares: "In the beginning was the Word, and the Word was with God, and the Word was God" (John 1:1).

When God speaks, He is actually sending forth part of Himself. When He speaks a specific thing, it carries the very essence of God because it is part of God. When He speaks something into existence, it comes to life in the realm of the spirit and remains there eternally alive. It throbs with all the power of God's eternal life just waiting for faith to get hold of it. When that word is sown in our hearts, it reproduces the life that spoke it into existence.

For example, Second Corinthians 5:17 says,

Therefore, if anyone is in Christ, he is [not will be] a new creation; old things have [already] *passed away;* [here is your past perfect tense] *behold, all things have [already] become new* (2 Corinthians 5:17).

Notice the tense in which these Scriptures are written. Imagine a few people who have just become believers. One is on drugs and is full of fear. Another may be 300 pounds overweight and completely unable to get up in the morning. Their lives are a mess in every sense. You look at them and say, "*Now where is this new creation in Christ?*" The answer is that this new creation already exists in the realm of the spirit. They have already been remade, and God has already spoken a totally new life into reality. Although it does not yet show in their earthly life, a glorious new person already exists in the heavenly realm.

When we are born again, God takes the *sperma* (the word translated "seed" in First Peter 1:23) of His Son and plants it into the womb of our spirit. Both men and women have a spiritual womb. In this way, God creates in us a new person that has our personality but also has the nature and life of God. When God has finished His good work in us, we are going to have our humanity impregnated with God's incorruptible nature.

Before we were even born physically and temporarily impaired with sin, God had already seen beyond this brief interlude to the glorious new creations that we would become in Christ. He saw us free from sin, with our humanity totally infused by the very nature of the living God. By the power of God, I can be as "Christ-like" as Jesus.

This is already done in the realm of the spirit because God has already spoken it into existence. For this to be manifested on Earth, you have to get hold of it by faith and bring it from the spiritual realm into this material time-space world. When you get hold of it by faith, the word becomes flesh in you in the same way that the word was made flesh in Jesus.

All that God has ever said is as eternally alive today as on the day that He spoke it. He spoke each word as an eternal word, and time does not affect it. It always remains fresh and powerful. It may be six thousand years old, but it is throbbing with the same glorious eternal life that it had when it first left the mouth of God and became self-existent as part of the great word of the living God.

Romans 4:17 shows all this in the life of Abraham. God spoke when Abraham was childless and impotent, and Sarah was barren. There was no hope naturally for these two to have even one child, not to mention a multitude. Yet God said to them, "I have made you a father of many nations, in the presence of Him whom he believed—God, who gives life to the dead and calls those things which [are not and they are]! (see Rom. 4:17, literally translated).

Unfortunately, in some translations, some English unbelief has crept in here. The New King James Version says it this way:

(as it is written, "I have made you a father of many nations") in the presence of Him whom he believed—God,

*who gives life to the dead and calls those things which
do not exist as though they did* (Romans 4:17).

I do not like the English translation "as *though* they did."
In Greek, this verse has the powerful image of stark urgency
like a newspaper-boy calling out the headlines. There is
urgency and excitement in what is being said, *God calls things
which are not into existence out of nothing, and they are!*

God does not need anything to make something. God
can create out of nothing. If you say, "God, I don't have anything," that does not bother God. He can start with nothing
and speak into existence the things which are not. The New
American Standard Bible translates it as follows:

*(as it is written, "A father of many nations have I made
you") in the presence of Him whom he believed, even
God, who gives life to the dead **and calls into being
that which does not exist*** (Romans 4:17 NASB).

God takes what is not, and suddenly it is, just by His
speaking! He does not need a little bit of something to
already exist in order to turn it into a lot of something. Even
if you are completely without discipline, He can speak discipline into your life. If there is no trace of holiness in your
life, He can still create it out of nothing. If you are the
biggest mess there ever was, He can speak the totally new
creation in Christ into existence, and it comes forth. You may
have had the most horrendous background. You may have
been abused all your life. You could have been told all your
life that you are no good, just a piece of rubbish. But God
says, "*You are pure. You are my cherished, beloved virgin in
Christ. I will transform you into something precious, powerful,
and valuable.*"

He speaks, and it is! But you have to get hold of that word by faith. Then, what He has already said becomes material substance in your life and you experience, through the activity of faith, what the word had already said.

Chapter 2

THE SOURCE OF FAITH

Paul gave Timothy three instructions:

1. Fight the good fight of faith.

2. Lay hold on eternal life, to which you were also called.

3. Maintain the good confession you made before many witnesses (see 1 Timothy 6:12-14).

We have covered the first command at length, so we will turn to the important statement in the second command: "Lay hold on eternal life, to which you were also called...." (1 Tim. 6:12). Paul tells Timothy to lay hold. The root Greek word here is *lambano*, which means "to strongly grasp hold of." Nothing comes to passive Christians. If you sit there praying and passively waiting for God to do something upon you, you can pray and wait forever. That is the fatalism of Hinduism, not Christianity. In Christianity there has to be a working together with God. Eternal life only becomes a reality in your life when you strongly grab hold of it.

There is a definite article in this command that is not present in all English translations. In the Greek, Paul very specifically tells Timothy to lay hold on *the* eternal life. *The eternal life is God's life.* We have to understand that only God has the ability to believe and move in real faith. God has perfect faith concerning His word and never doubts that what He has spoken will come to pass. The life of God throbs with that perfect faith. He is completely confident that He is able to bring to pass every word He has ever said. He knows He can do it. God by His very nature is the perfect believer, and He cannot doubt. God never wakes up on a Monday morning and says, *Oh, goodness Me, why did I say that? How am I ever going to make that happen?*

Not only does God Himself live by His perfect faith, but He has declared that "the just shall live by his faith" (Hab. 2:4). It is outside human ability and beyond human nature to come to faith. If we do not understand this, we will spend the rest of our lives unsuccessfully struggling to move in faith. We cannot manufacture faith. The only way we can be a man or woman of faith is to receive it from God. This is why Paul instructed Timothy to "*take hold* of the eternal life to which you were called" (1 Tim. 6:12 NASB). It is not something we work up, but something we grab hold of.

HAVE GOD'S FAITH

Mark 11:22 is a key verse concerning faith. Peter had just observed the withering of the fig tree which Jesus had cursed the previous day. With amazement, Peter remarked, "*Rabbi look! The fig tree which You cursed has shriveled up and died!*" (see Mark 11:21).

In most English manuscripts Jesus' answer is written down as "Have faith in God" (Mark 11:22). Unfortunately, this is a poor translation of the Greek. *Theou,* the Greek word for God here, is in the genitive case, indicating that faith is a possession of God. It is the faith that belongs to God. In addition, the verb "have" is in the passive voice, which means we have to actively receive something coming to us from an external source, namely God Himself.

Imagine that Eileen, my wife, picks up my Bible and says to you, "Here, have Alan's Bible." This would be in the genitive case. Putting the word Bible in the genitive case would indicate that she is giving to you the Bible that belongs to Alan. Alan's Bible is being offered to you, and the appropriate response would be to reach out and take hold of Alan's Bible so that it becomes yours.

That is what Jesus was saying here. Jesus was not commanding His disciples to somehow manufacture faith by their own efforts. He knew they could not generate faith themselves. Jesus was saying, *Listen, God is the perfect believer. He already has perfect faith and is willing to give it to you as a free gift. If you learn how to receive, you will have God's faith. With His faith, you can speak to mountains and move them out of the way, or like Me, you can speak to fig trees, and they will immediately die.*

By laying hold of His eternal life, God's faith comes to us. His eternal life in us fills us with His faith and makes us believers like God. We cannot do it for ourselves, but God can work in us and bring us to His faith. True faith believes God's word the way God believes it. If you take hold of the eternal life to which you were called, then you will find God's life being poured into you. God's life pouring into you produces God's life in you, and God's life in you has the ability to believe without doubting what God has said. When you have come to fullness here, then God's word in your mouth becomes the same as God's word in God's mouth. That is what it means to have God's faith.

This is how Jesus lived. He cursed the fig tree by the faith of God, and it died. God had given His faith to His Son as a life-flow. Jesus said, *I live by the Father. The Father is My life. I have His eternal life that lives in Me and flows out of Me. This eternal life enables Me to believe like God.*

God lives by faith, and the eternal life of God is the perfect faith life. That is why to be compatible with God, and in order to please God, you have to live a life of faith like Him. If you do not live by faith, you and God become incompatible.

RECEIVING FAITH

Jesus said, "Have God's faith!" (See Mark 11:22.) You will never get there by trying to make yourself believe. This is why the second statement in First Timothy 6 is so important: "Take hold of the eternal life to which you were called…" (1 Tim. 6:12 NASB). The more you fill yourself up with God's life and God's Word, the more you fill yourself up with God's ability to believe God's Word.

The verb "have" is in the passive voice (see Mark 11:22). When a verb is in the passive voice, it means that the subject of the sentence needs to receive something. It means that something from outside comes to you. You are the beneficiary of the action of someone or something else toward you.

However, the English word "passive" doesn't really describe this tense. In order for this action toward you to be effective, there has to be an activity within you to receive what's being done to you. If you get into real inactive passivity then you are in Hinduism or Islam, not Christianity. *"It is the will of Allah, and I can't do anything about it."* Many evangelicals are really fatalists. They have such an overemphasis on the sovereignty of God that they live in total, inactive passivity. That is not what is being taught here. We must actively "cooperate" with God. God is the initiator, the supplier, the provider, but there has to be an activity of receiving on our part from within us.

Everyone in the Bible who was baptized by the Holy Spirit was a person who received the Holy Spirit. The Holy Spirit never fell on individuals and hit them on the head when they weren't seeking and expecting it. Revival will never come anywhere by us passively waiting for God to fall on the place. There has to be a way in which we work together with God.

The same word is used repeatedly about receiving the Holy Spirit. Some people are so tight they can't receive. It's like a man saying, "I'm thirsty! I'm thirsty!" but he keeps his mouth tightly shut. Someone brings him a big glass of water and tries to pour it into his mouth, but he keeps his mouth shut, and the water runs down his shirt, and he doesn't actually drink any of it.

I had an immense problem being filled with the Holy Spirit. The night that Eileen was gloriously baptized in the Holy Spirit we finally got home and went to bed. As we lay in bed I said, "Lord, it's wonderful what You did to Eileen, but we are married, and we always do everything together. Please come to me as You have come to her." Then in the middle of the night, the room filled up with the presence of God. When I felt the room fill up with the presence of God something inside me shut down. I was so hungry, and yet I was scared. I didn't move physically, but in my inner man I shut down and wouldn't let God come. The moment I did that, God removed Himself.

Suddenly the place felt so desolate. I thought, "Lord, I've prayed for a whole year for this, and then when You come, I'm frightened. Forgive me. I don't understand myself. Please give me another chance."

About 15 to 20 minutes later the room again filled up with God's presence again. This time I wasn't going to miss it! So in my inner man I leaped at Him. I was still lying in bed. I didn't move physically, but I was so determined not to miss Him again that I leaped at Him in my spirit and tried to grab Him. However, God won't be snatched at, and He withdrew Himself again. Then the word came to me, which is there in the Bible so many times, "yield." God was training me how to receive. The third time God's presence filled the room, I didn't run away from Him, and I didn't snatch at Him. I just lay there and let Him come, and, as best I knew how, I opened myself to Him.

The two things that hit me were how holy He is and how much He loved Alan Vincent. God loves to come and love you. I've learned to be a good receiver. Intimacy is the key to coming to great faith. If you cannot be intimate with God, then you cannot be a good receiver. If you are unable to receive, then you will be unable to partake of all that God has for you.

Then Jesus said to Peter,

Whoever says to this mountain, "Be removed and be cast into the sea," and does not doubt in his heart, but believes that those things he says will be done, he will have whatever he says. Therefore I say to you, whatever things you ask when you pray, believe that you receive them, and you will have them (Mark 11:23-24).

Once you receive God's faith and God's undoubting eternal life is filling you, then it is natural for you to believe like God. You will simply do what Jesus did.

There is a vast treasure house full of all the things that God has said, but none will be manifested in your life unless you start acting in faith. If you learn to move in faith, then you can have them all. Hebrews 11:6 says,

But without faith it is impossible to please Him, for he who comes to God must believe that He is, and that He is a rewarder of those who diligently seek Him (Hebrews 11:6).

This is a strong statement. You have to believe what God says and that He will reward you as you seek Him. I suggest that you write down, "*I'm going to believe that this will work for me.*" If you step out and personalize this teaching, then it will work for you. It worked for Paul, and he desperately wanted to impart this to Timothy. Romans 10:17 tells us, "Faith comes by hearing, and hearing by the Word of God."

Notice that it is hearing the Word of God and not just reading it. You have to hear God speaking these things into your heart with your spiritual ears attentive to God and your spiritual eyes wide open. It has to come alive for you.

This verse says, "Faith comes by hearing the *rhematos* (the specific spoken word) about the Christ." You have to hear God say the particular word that you personally need at that time so that you can confidently say, *"I've heard it, I've seen it, and now I know that I know. I've got the title deed for that particular word."* General information about God's Word does not produce faith. Instead, faith comes as you hear God speak to you precept by precept and word by word.

First Corinthians 2:9-13 tells us that because we have received the Spirit of God, we can know with certainty the things that God has freely given us. We don't have to guess.

> *Now we have received, not the spirit of the world, but the Spirit who is from God, that we might know the things that have been freely given to us by God* (1 Corinthians 2:12).

When you need to be healed, you need God to specifically speak to you that you are healed. It is not sufficient to believe that God *can* heal because you have read it in Scripture or have heard someone teach it. It is not enough that your friend has experienced healing. You have to hear God say it to you personally. You do not get the title deed for the whole of Scripture at one time, but specific words for specific things enable you to grow from one level of faith to another.

THE WRITTEN WORD

The primary source for hearing God is the written word of Scripture. The fruit of God's Word is to bring God's life into you, word by word and phrase by phrase, until all that God is comes to fullness in you. All that God is, you can find in His Word. He is the great *Logos*! God breaks the whole *logos* into specific *rhema* words, which He speaks into your heart. When that word comes to harvest, it produces in you the very source that spoke it. Because all that God is can be found in His Word, it can never be irrelevant, it can never grow old, and it can never fail. The totality of "who God is" is in His Word!

We must read the Word of God with the hearing of faith. Many people read God's Word and filter it through their rational intellect, their experiences, and their current circumstances. They pick and choose what to believe and apply to their lives what seems to makes sense to them rather than choosing to believe everything God says in His Word.

In Galatians 3:2 Paul asks,

This only I want to learn from you: Did you receive the Spirit by the works of the law, or by the hearing of faith?

The answer is obviously by the hearing of faith. You have to hear God's Word and say, "*I believe that and I receive that.*" Being filled with the Holy Spirit is a matter of faith. Getting saved is a matter of faith. You have to hear the Word of God and then get hold of it by faith.

The main source of faith is the written Word of God, but we have to hear it or see it in our spirit (or our heart) in order to truly receive these things. We can memorize Scripture and yet still not be able to move in faith because it has never become truly revealed in our heart. It is crucial that we understand what the Word of God is and how to handle the Word of God in this respect. Many people memorize Scripture, and yet it never helps them to move in faith because they have never been able to approach Scripture with the hearing of faith.

Galatians 3:5 adds,

Therefore He who supplies the Spirit to you and works miracles among you, does He do it by the works of the law, or by the hearing of faith?

The hearing of faith allows the Holy Spirit to live in you continually and causes miracles to take place through you. It is not enough just to be in an atmosphere of faith; the faith must be in you. James 5:15 declares that *"the prayer of faith will save the sick"* (James 5:15). Prayer alone does not heal the sick, but the prayer of faith does. Prayer without faith is just a religious exercise that accomplishes nothing.

THE VOICE OF GOD

The primary source for faith is hearing the word of God in Scripture. However, God can also speak powerfully to us through genuine prophets and the prophetic gift. We can also hear God speak directly to us by His Spirit in our hearts. Both of these later categories are much harder to define and carry a certain danger of being misused. However, through them God can and does speak faith into us in a powerful way.

We have probably all known some Christians who have believed they heard God speak to them when they had actually made it up presumptuously in their own imagination. We must not become cynical, but we do need to follow the biblical safeguards, test everything in this category, and then hold fast only to that which is good (see 1 Thess. 5:19-21).

In some very significant moments in my life, God has spoken directly to me. One example happened some years ago when I had returned from India to lead a group of churches in England. Mandy was a 24-year-old woman in one of our churches, the same age as my daughter Rachel at that time. Mandy had given birth to a little baby, but five months later she developed an acute form of Hodgkin's disease. This cancer attacked her lymph glands and then began to spread to other parts of her body. We had already seen some wonderful healings in our churches, so we formed a "commando prayer group" to fight for Mandy's life.

We prayed earnestly for her healing, but we could not break through to victory. In the end, Mandy tragically died. Within a few hours of her death, her husband Andy called me and said, "Alan, I don't feel at peace to just go and bury Mandy's body. Maybe God is taking us to the limit. Would you come and pray with me over Mandy's body to see whether God will raise her from the dead?"

Mandy's body was in one of the major London hospitals. The hospital authorities were very cooperative, and they put Mandy's body in the private chapel in the hospital and allowed us to go and pray. The four of us spent a whole afternoon praying over her. It was an incredible experience. The presence of God in that room was very intense. We were worshipping and feeling so exhilarated in our spirits. It seemed the easiest and most natural thing in the world just to turn to Mandy's body and say, "Mandy, get up!"

So I turned and spoke to her and said, "Mandy, get up in Jesus' name." But she didn't get up. Instead, God spoke very clearly to me in my spirit. This is what He said, *"You don't know how near you came, but there are still some more things you have to learn before you can see this kind of victory. I want you to see this defeat like an Olympic high jumper tipping the bar just one centimeter short of the Olympic record. You came that close. You almost got the gold medal, but there are reasons, which I cannot explain to you now, why I had to concede this to the devil. It was not my perfect will for Mandy to die. This was satan's malice, and he's going to have to pay for it. As compensation I am going to give you a hundredfold return for Mandy's life."*

I heard God say this. There is no verse in Scripture that says anything like this, but I heard God speak these words to me, and they became an absolute word of faith to me. In that moment I received a "faith check" for a hundred people's lives that the devil would otherwise have been able to kill. I had no idea that only a few months later I was going to be cashing the first installment of that heavenly check.

At that time my daughter Rachel and her husband Gordon Hickson were visiting a Reinhard Bonnke crusade in Harare, Zimbabwe, wondering if this was where God would have them serve. The crusade had just concluded with amazing results. Powerful witchdoctors were saved, and they brought vast amounts of witchcraft paraphernalia to be burned. There was such intense satanic activity that the drums which had been used for demonic incantations were physically leaping out of the fire refusing to be burned. They had to stake down the drums in the fire in order to burn them.

Outside the home where Rachel, Gordon, and the team were staying, two wide roads converged at a major intersection. That evening the visibility was perfect, and there were no unusual weather patterns, yet all of sudden two major car crashes took place at this junction due to the demonic activity.

The first wreck involved an important Zimbabwe government official. He crashed into the back of his own police escort vehicle, which had stopped to make a turn. He himself was impaled on the steering wheel, and the security guards in the back of his car were seriously injured.

When Rachel and Gordon heard the noise of the accident, they ran out to try to help the injured. They had just begun prying open the front door where this man was impaled on the steering wheel when a heavy military truck ran into the already-existing wreck. My daughter was crushed between the two vehicles as they were pushed some distance down the road due to the force of the impact. She was seriously injured and had many fractures to both legs. Gordon had spinal injuries, and his pelvis was broken in several places. Since there was no ambulance service in Zimbabwe, they got Rachel and Gordon out of the wreck and transported them to the hospital in an ordinary car.

Reinhard Bonnke called me by phone in England to inform me of the accident and the condition of Rachel and Gordon. His first report was that they were stable. Although they had been badly injured, it looked like they were going to be all right.

Eileen and I made plans to go out to be with them in Harare. But, after two days Reinhard called again and said, "You'd better come quickly! Rachel has fallen into a coma!" Immediately we drove to the airport to catch the first plane out with only ten minutes to spare. I actually wrote the check for the ticket on the side of the plane as we were boarding. This was the only flight that flew directly to Harare in the next two or three days. During the night, the devil came and attacked me as I sat on the plane and said, "*She will be dead by the time you get there.*"

Then God spoke to me, "*Cash the check! The one I gave you over Mandy's death.*" Immediately I came to faith, and I said to the devil, "No! Rachel is not going to die. Instead, this is the first payment you will have to make for what you did to Mandy. This is my first claim!"

I never imagined I would be using this "check" first of all for Rachel's life. We flew all night and rushed straight to the hospital the next morning to be with Rachel. By the time we got there, she had been in a coma for three or four days. The medical consultant, a Russian expert, said to me, "She has a five percent chance of survival, but there will be such extensive brain damage that it would be better for her to die."

I said, "No! God has told me that she is going to live and that she will be normal." We prayed all day. Other great people came to pray. Reinhard himself came to pray. I was certainly not the sole intercessor in this affair. Much prayer was made for Rachel.

That evening we saw the first glimmer of response in her body. She began to come out of her deep coma. She spoke and said she was thirsty. She also said she was hot. These were the first signs of contact with her. By this time I was utterly exhausted, and I fell asleep in the chair beside her bed.

The next morning, Rachel woke up. Mentally she was perfectly fine. Against all medical odds, she had absolutely no brain damage. However, her legs were still badly broken and twisted, and one was severely shortened.

Over the next four years, Rachel experienced a series of miracles through various people's prayers that brought her back to complete wholeness. If you saw her now, you would see a perfectly normal woman without a trace of the severe injuries to her body. God totally and completely restored her.

In the years that followed Rachel's accident, we saw several people diagnosed with terminal cancer. There was no hope for them naturally, yet all of them were healed. Since that time, I have seen the most amazing miracles all around the world. I have seen at least a hundredfold return for Mandy's life.

This shows how you can hear a word of God that is not explicitly written in the Bible. If you have truly heard God speak into your spirit, then you can cash checks of faith based on the word you have heard. While the Bible is the main source for hearing a word of faith, it is not the only one. The important thing is to make sure you have genuinely heard God speak and that you do not interpret your own desires and wishes as a word from God.

If you get hold of God's life, then God's faith comes as part of the package. Therefore, God's life must increasingly fill you. You must live by His life and not your own. When His life becomes your life, and the power and energy of your life is truly the eternal life of the living God, then faith will be as natural to you as it is to God. The more you are filled with God's life, the more you find yourself being moved to think like God and speak like God. You will find that the power of God's eternal life fills you with faith.

BE PERSUADABLE

I want to look more closely at a couple things from Romans 4. God chooses His examples in Scripture very carefully. For example, God deliberately took Jacob to show us what He can do with the most unpromising natural material. Esau, Jacob's brother, was a much more likable person and was Isaac's favorite son. He was athletic and handsome and today would have been the quarterback on the college football team. He would have looked fantastic and been well liked by everyone. Jacob, however, was a weak, sickly, unathletic, and unpopular kind of boy, and he was his mother's pet. Nevertheless, Jacob wanted God, and he was prepared to use all the deceptive power and cunning of his twisted nature to get his spiritual heritage. God saw his heart and not his methodology and said, "Jacob I have loved, but Esau I have hated" (Rom. 9:13).

The self-sufficient Esau with all of his natural ability and self-confidence was not interested in God. God does not merely dislike self-sufficiency, He hates it. God took Jacob and turned him into a prince with both God and man. He made him into the patriarch of His entire chosen nation. By choosing Jacob as his scriptural example, God is clearly saying that if He can do such a transforming work with someone like Jacob, then no one is too hard for Him, and He can certainly transform you and me.

God did a similar thing with Abraham. He did not have a natural ability for faith. In fact before God started to change him, Abraham was chronically unbelieving, and God had to bring him to faith. Faith is not a talent that some have and others don't. Some people reason that way and say, "She has the gift of faith, and I don't." They look at faith in the same way they look at other abilities, such as playing the piano, painting, or negotiating a business deal. Faith is not like that at all! No one has the natural ability to believe like

God. Faith is not a talent in the natural sense. It is contrary to our natural disposition and is a gift that comes from God. The Spirit of God imparts the faith of God through our participation with God's life.

When God told Abraham, "You will have a child in your old age," Abraham laughed. He was already 100 years old, and Sarah was 90, well beyond child-bearing years. She had been barren since he married her. He also was now impotent. These two dried-up prunes had no chance in the natural of producing anything. Yet, regardless of how impossible it was in the natural, Abraham remained persuadable.

Unfortunately, the New King James Version and a number of other English Bibles translate Romans 4 in an unsatisfactory way as follows:

> *And not being weak in faith, he did **not** consider his own body, already dead (since he was about a hundred years old), and the deadness of Sarah's womb. He did not waver at the promise of God through unbelief, but was strengthened in faith, giving glory to God, and being fully convinced that what He had promised He was also able to perform* (Romans 4:19–21).

This version says that Abraham did not consider his own body or the deadness of Sarah's womb. But the truth is that Abraham squarely faced the fact that his body was as good as dead and that Sarah's womb was also dead, and he still chose to believe God and remain persuadable, believing that He could still do it. Scholars such as Kenneth Wuest, Marvin Vincent, and others all agree that the best manuscripts omit the negative before "considered" in verse 19 and that the best translation should be as it is in the New American Standard Bible:

> *Without becoming weak in faith he contemplated his own body, now as good as dead since he was about a hundred years old, and the deadness of Sarah's womb; yet, with respect to the promise of God, he did not waver in unbelief but grew strong in faith, giving glory to God, and being fully assured that what God had promised, He was able also to perform* (Romans 4:19–21 NASB).

Abraham did not kid himself. He recognized that it was totally impossible naturally, yet Abraham did not decide against God but remained persuadable. When God empowered him with supernatural faith, he was then able to be fully convinced by God that He could do it.

God will bring you to faith if you are persuadable. Even if you are completely lacking in faith, if you remain persuadable and do not decide against God, He can empower you with His faith and transform you just as He did Abraham. Determine not to reason against the promises of God through unbelief but to remain persuadable. Then by the infusion of His life, which is full of His faith, you will become fully convinced that God is able to fulfill His promise to you.

CHAPTER 3

THE CRIPPLING POWER OF UNBELIEF

GOD HATES UNBELIEF

God cannot stand unbelief. He does not just dislike unbelief; He actually hates it! If you read through the Gospels, you will notice that the one thing that stirred up righteous anger in Jesus was unbelief. It was the only reason Jesus ever gave for His disciples' failure. The Scriptures only give one reason for powerlessness and that is that we simply do not have the faith.

Paul first instructed Timothy to "Fight the good fight of faith," and then went on to explain that Timothy was to lay hold of the eternal life to which he had been called (see 1 Tim. 6:12). If you get filled with God's life, then you also get filled with God's faith.

Before I was saved, I called myself a scientific atheist. My wife and I had not been churchgoers, but on the day we were saved, we began to read the Bible and decided simply to believe it. From the first day of our new life in Christ, miracles began to happen. Unfortunately, we moved after a few weeks and began going to a church that was not experiencing anything miraculous and did not believe in the miraculous. This atmosphere slowly sowed a veil of unbelief over my mind. I could no longer do the things I did when I was freshly saved. It is amazing how fast that evil spirit of religious unbelief grabs hold of people.

We went to India and worked amongst evangelical missionaries with no miraculous power working through their lives. Although they knew the Scriptures, they were bound up by legalism and law. However, God graciously visited a few of us; we were baptized in the Holy Spirit, and everything began to change.

STILL NOT BELIEVING FOR JOY AND AMAZEMENT

Some years later, Eileen and I returned to England for a few months, and I agreed to pastor a small church while I was home. In this church was a middle-aged woman with teenage children. She suddenly telephoned me one day and said, "Alan, I have just had some very bad news, and I need you to come round and pray for me."

I got into my car and drove to this lady's house. As I was driving to her house, I kept wondering about a strange feeling in my arms. It was the first time I had ever felt it. My arms were feeling heavy, and there was a strange tingle at the same time. It was what I now know to be the power of God.

I got to her house and went in, and she told me her story. About eighteen months earlier, some strange things had begun to happen in her body. She had suddenly started to grow again and was already one inch taller than she used to be. Her feet and her hands had grown larger, and she had to buy new shoes and gloves several sizes larger. Then her legs began to get unsteady, and her eyesight began to be affected. She had just been to see a consultant in London, and he had diagnosed that there was a malignant tumor pressing on her pituitary gland. The prognosis was very bad as it was impossible to operate successfully to remove it. She had been given only a short time to live. She said, "Alan, I want you to pray for me."

I knew very little about moving in the power of God. I could pray prayers of sympathy, but I did not know how to pray prayers of faith. I stood in front of this woman, reached out my hands toward her, and began to pray. As I just touched her, she immediately fell backward on the floor under the power of God. I had never seen this happen before. She cried out, "Oh!" And I said, "What happened?" She said, "I felt myself shrink!"

After a few minutes, she got up from the floor and said, "My legs are absolutely steady. My eyesight is perfect." Then she left the room to get a pair of her older, smaller shoes. When she put them on, they fit her feet perfectly! In a fraction of a second, she had shrunk back to her original size. This miracle was confirmed later by the same consultant she had seen before. Every trace of that condition just disappeared from her body, and it has never returned. Hallelujah!

As I sat there looking at this woman I was feeling a kind of joy inside me, but at the same time I was filled with dumb unbelief. I saw this miracle with my own eyes. I felt the power go through me, yet the first thing I heard myself saying to her was, "This is wonderful, but I can't believe that it has happened!" God had used me as a channel of His power and had healed her in a fraction of a second before my eyes, but I still could not believe it had happened.

I suddenly began to understand the strange and unbelievable behavior of the disciples on resurrection morning when they refused to believe all the evidence and even the testimonies that Jesus was risen. They point-blank refused to believe, even though He had told them many times before-hand that it would happen exactly the way it did. When Jesus finally appeared before all of them in the upper room, Luke records that "they still did not believe it because of joy and amazement" (Luke 24:41 NIV).

I knew exactly what this meant because I was experiencing the same thing. I said, "God, what is the matter with me?" He said, "Unbelief!" God took me to Hebrews 3:12, which addresses "brethren," not unbelievers.

See to it, brothers, that none of you has a sinful, unbelieving heart that turns away from the living God (Hebrews 3:12 NIV).

That morning God said to me, "Alan, you are one of these brethren. If you don't deal with this, spiritually, you will die in the wilderness and never come into your inheritance." Unbelief is not simply the absence of faith; it is much worse than that. It is an activity against God. My respectable, rational, and scientific heart contained a great mountain of stubborn unbelief that would not believe, even when I saw things with my own eyes.

I said to God, "This is terrible!" and cried out to be delivered from that evil spirit. I did not feel the demon leave me, nor was there any demonic manifestation, but it did leave, and the power of unbelief in my life was broken from that very moment. That day I began to hate unbelief the way God hates it. I also made a decision never to allow such devilish, unbelieving thoughts to occupy my mind ever again.

TWO KINDS OF UNBELIEF

In the Greek language there are two words for unbelief. The first word is *apisteuo* which means "the inability to cling to, to cast yourself in reliance upon, or the inability to stick to like glue." All of us naturally have this inability. This is normal human nature. It is weak, not wicked. It tries to believe, but it can't.

In Mark 9:18–24, the father of the demoniac boy, who met Jesus as He came down from the mount of transfiguration, said, "Jesus, if you can do anything then please help me!" Jesus replied "If I can do anything? If you can believe! All things are possible to him who believes." Then the father cried out, "Oh, Lord, I believe, but help my unbelief." (See Mark 9:18-24.) This is the normal confession of human nature. God was not angry with this type of unbelief. He is not angry because you cannot believe. However, God does get angry if you refuse to be persuaded. God does get angry if you are determined not to believe.

This brings me to the second Greek word, which is *apeitheo*. This word means "to decide against, to refuse to be persuaded, to be non-compliant, to make a definite, willful decision against." This kind of unbelief is stubborn, determined, and wicked—not just weak. God hates it because it always leads to disobedience.

Apeitheo is used in Hebrews 3:18 when it says that the children of Israel died in the wilderness because they would not believe that God could take them into the promised land. (See Hebrews 3:16-19.) They said, "*This is crazy. We will not believe it. Don't even talk to us about it. There is no way!*"

This same word is used in John 3:36 where it says,

He who believes [pisteuo] in the Son has everlasting life; and he who does not believe [apeitheo—i.e., makes the determined decision not to believe] *the Son shall not see life, but the wrath of God abides on him* (John 3:36).

The same word (apeitheo) is sometimes translated "disobedience" in the New Testament because that is always the practical result. However, God can always bring anyone to faith, provided they are persuadable.

Come back to Romans 4:20-22:

He [Abraham] *did not waver at the promise of God through unbelief, but was strengthened in faith, giving glory to God, and being fully convinced that what He had promised He was also able to perform. And therefore, "it was accounted to him for righteousness."*

It says that Abraham did not waver at the promise. The literal Greek translation says this, "against the promise of God he did not decide by unbelief." Essentially, Abraham said, *"God, I don't know how You can give us a child in our old age. I don't see how I could possibly be the father of nations. I don't see how I could have descendents as numerous as the sands of the sea or as numerous as the stars in heaven. But, I will not say You can't do it."* This was all God needed to bring Abraham to faith. God will understand and continue to work with us when it is a matter of the weakness of human unbelief, but not when it is a matter of a person's stubborn, willful decision not to believe.

Then it says in verse 20 that Abraham "was strengthened in faith" (Rom. 4:20). This phrase is in the passive voice. The passive voice means that the subject of a sentence has something done to it and remains the passive beneficiary of what is done to it. A good translation is this, "Abraham was empowered (or dynamited) with faith."

PARADOX OF BIBLICAL PASSIVITY

At this point I need to explain the paradox of biblical passivity, which frequently occurs in Scripture, so that we can stay in the balance of truth. In the Greek language every verb is grammatically written in one of three possible voices. One is called the passive voice.

When this passive voice is used, it means that the subject of the sentence is having something done to it or imparted to it from an external source by the object of the sentence. But this does not mean passivity in the sense of non-responsive inertness. In fact it is usually necessary for the beneficiary to be active in receiving what is being offered to him.

For example, you could be dying of thirst, and someone comes and offers you a drink. You gratefully and actively receive it, gulp it down, and are refreshed. Because you are the recipient of this external benefit, the verb "receive" in Greek would be written in the passive voice even though you actively took what was being offered to you and gulped it down.

When it comes to faith, God Himself is the only real source of genuine faith. It is impossible for any human being to generate real faith from within themselves. You have to be empowered by God to believe just like Abraham, Sarah, and even Paul were. But we must be actively open and receiving in our response in order for this supernatural impartation to take place.

When you go to the dentist, it is good to be passive. The dentist does not expect you to do anything except open your mouth and "cooperate" with him. He does the rest. Psalm 81:10 says, "Open thy mouth wide, and I will fill it says the Lord" (KJV).

All you need to do is submit yourself to God and open your mouth. He will drill out every negative thing you say and think until all the negative attitudes and words are removed from your mind and your vocabulary. Don't ever say, "*I'm no good. I'll never make it. This place will never change. I tried all this, and it didn't work.*" Get all that unbelief out!

Before God can give you the positive, He must deal with the negative.

> *But the righteousness of faith speaks in this way, "Do not say in your heart, 'Who will ascend into heaven?'" (that is, to bring Christ down from above) or, "'Who will descend into the abyss?'" (that is, to bring Christ up from the dead). But what does it say? "The word is near you, in your mouth and in your heart" (that is, the word of faith which we preach)* (Romans 10:6-8).

The word is in your mouth and heart so that you can do it! Real faith does not begin by saying certain things, but it begins by *not saying* certain things. You make a decision not to confess the negative unbelief that the devil is trying to feed you. Once God has drilled all the negative out of your mouth, He can fill you with the positive truth of God, which then becomes golden faith in your mouth.

This is what happened to Abraham. He sat in the divine dentist chair, and God empowered him with faith. He sat there passively as God changed his mouth. When God finished with him, he was no longer laughing with unbelief, but believed God's word as much as God did. He was a passive beneficiary of God's faith-filled life. It says in verse 21 that after God was finished with him, Abraham became fully convinced that what God had said He was well able to perform, and therefore, it was accounted to him for righteousness (see Rom. 4:21-22).

This was when Isaac was conceived. It took God 25 years to bring Abraham to this place of faith, but He got him there. Sarah had to be brought to faith as well before she could conceive. It says in Hebrews 11:11 that Sarah was empowered (or dynamited) into faith in order to have the power to conceive (see Heb. 11:11). It took dynamite to bring her out of her barrenness, but God did it!

RELIGIOUS UNBELIEF

There are two major institutions used by the devil to promote unbelief. One form comes to us through the various religious systems many of us were exposed to in our childhood. This was particularly true of the religious system established by the scribes and Pharisees in Jerusalem in Jesus' day. When He went back to His own hometown of Nazareth, after he was empowered with the Holy Spirit, His home synagogue violently rejected Him and even tried to kill

Him. We read that He marveled at their unbelief and could do no miracle there (see Mark 6:1-6).

Second Corinthians 3:14-18 speaks of those who were raised under Moses' law: "Even to this day, when Moses is read, a veil covers their hearts" (see 2 Cor. 3:15). This veil is not natural, but supernatural. The god of religion has blinded their minds so that when they read the Scriptures they cannot see Jesus in them.

A day is coming when this veil will suddenly be removed, and the Jews will see what they ought to have seen centuries ago. Being soaked in Moses' law and the religious rules they created makes it almost impossible for Jews to believe in Jesus. This puzzled me for years because the Jewish religion was given by God, and if any religion has the power to save, it should have been the Jewish religion

God gave this "perfect religion" for two purposes. First, to show that even the best of religions cannot save no matter how good it is. Second, it was meant to equip people to recognize Christ easily when He came. Instead, the devil wove a thick veil of unbelief around Judaism, particularly at its center in Jerusalem, making it impossible for them to see Jesus and believe until that veil is miraculously taken away. One of the most important prayers we can pray for Orthodox Jews is, "Lord, let that veil be removed!"

At the height of the Davidic kingdom, during the first years of King Solomon, the Jews were trading everywhere (see 1 Kings 10). People came from great distances to this fantastic kingdom because people everywhere were giving testimony of its greatness. The Queen of Sheba came and was so astonished at what she saw that she took Judaism back to Ethiopia. Many Ethiopians became Jewish prose-lytes, and Jewish trading communities were established there.

The Jews also sent trading ships around the world, going as far as India. They would return after two or three years, rich with the treasures of India, bringing back goods such as ivory and peacocks. The Hebrew word for *ivory* is the Indian Tamil word, which means "the tooth of an elephant." The Hebrew word for *peacock* is also the Tamil word. The Hebrews did not have their own words for these things, so they adopted the Indian words into their language. As a result of this trading, Jews went to India and settled Jewish communities who established synagogues and permanent trading posts. Many local people were converted when they saw the superiority of Judaism compared with their own pagan idolatry.

In the Book of Acts, we see how Judaism did in fact prepare the way for Christ. A high official came from Ethiopia to Jerusalem. He was the secretary of Queen Candice of Ethiopia and a Jewish proselyte. As he journeyed to celebrate the Feast of Passover, he was reverently reading Isaiah chapter 53 but could not understand what it said. However, as soon as Philip began to preach to him, the Ethiopian immediately saw the truth. The veil of Moses was not over his eyes because he had not been brought up under the teaching of the scribes and Pharisees in Jerusalem. All he had was the Scriptures and the Holy Spirit, so as soon as he heard Philip, he cried out, "This is the fulfillment of Scripture!" and was immediately converted. He asked, "Why can't I be baptized?" and he was and went on his way rejoicing. (See Acts 8:26-40.) The scribes and Pharisees could not behave like this because the spirit of unbelief had blinded their minds.

Matthew went to Ethiopia to reach these "lost sheep of the house of Israel." A powerful move of the Holy Spirit took place, and thousands became believers. They had no problem seeing Jesus as the fulfillment of the Scriptures which they had already read. (See Matthew 10:1-8.)

About the same time, Thomas went to the Jewish communities in Kerala and Tamil Nadu in southern India. They had been trading with Israel for approximately 1,000 years. As Thomas preached, there was a powerful move of God, and many believed. Thomas was martyred by militant Hindus in A.D. 72 but not before a powerful church was established. This church badly apostatized, but has recently been powerfully revived and is now touching the whole nation.

These people had the Scriptures and the Jewish religion for centuries, and when Jesus was preaching, they could immediately see that He was the fulfillment of all they had been reading and anticipating. In contrast, the unbelieving behavior of Orthodox Jews is caused by a supernatural, demonic veil that covers their minds and blinds them from believing, even as they read the Scriptures. When that veil is removed, there will be a revolution amongst them.

In a similar way, Catholic churches, as well as many Lutheran, Baptist, Evangelical, and Pentecostal churches, have produced a religious blindness. Where there is law and legalism, this spirit comes and occupies religious activities and communities. A veil is sown by the devil so that Christianity becomes an exercise in obeying rules and regulations and not the powerful Gospel that brings freedom and empowerment.

SECULAR, RATIONAL UNBELIEF

Unbelief is also found in our secular, rational reason, which comes to us through our education system. Two major demonic principalities rule these streams of unbelief. One is the prince of false religion. Otherwise known as the prince of Persia, it is at the root and source of every false religion and wrong exploration of the spirit realm (such as New Age, spiritism, or any involvement with the occult). When we are captured in any way by false religions or philosophies, this spirit weaves unbelief over our minds so that we cannot believe.

The second spirit is the prince of Greece. That spirit is the evil spirit driving natural logic and reason of the secular mind. I was trained as a scientist in this way. Prior to becoming a Christian I was a successful scientist. I was trained to think very rationally and throw out anything that couldn't be explained by reason and science. The moment I got saved, I had an insatiable appetite to read the Bible. At that point in my life, I was lecturing in a College of Advanced Technology in Great Britain. It was early July, and lecturers stopped lecturing in June and did not start again until October. So Eileen went off to work every day, and, as we had no children, I just stayed home and read her Bible all day. I made notes, but I was intellectually rejecting many things as I went along: *That's just a silly myth. That's an impossible story. I can't believe that. But, some parts are actually quite good. I really like what Jesus said.* That was my attitude toward the Bible. When I got to Hebrews 11:3 in September, God stopped me, and three months after I was saved, I had this new encounter with God. He actually spoke to me, *"Alan, you're not going to get anywhere until you change your attitude toward My Word."*

He was so present I could hardly dare to speak, but I said, "What do you mean?" God then asked me, "*How did you come to receive Jesus?*" I replied, "I just made a decision to believe what the man who led me to Jesus said. I didn't understand the cross, but I just decided to believe it." God then said, "I want you to have the same attitude toward all My Word. Take all those doubts and every bit of the Bible that you decided you couldn't believe because of your intellect and throw them out of the window like trash and never let them in again."

God showed me that I had to totally change the way I thought about Scripture. That morning He rewired my mind to think like God. It was a sudden, dramatic experience. I wasn't persuaded by superior intellectual arguments to become a creationist rather than an evolutionist. I was ordered by God to believe it. Now I have masses of very good scientific evidence to support my faith, but at that time, it was just a blind step of faith. I didn't become a "God-thinker" by intellectual persuasion. I became a "God-thinker" by a miracle that renewed my mind. I haven't stopped using my mind, but I use it in a different way. I'm like a little child who just believes everything that God says and steps out to do things the way God says to do them. It's that simple.

In a moment I was delivered from years of intellectual western education, and I now think like God. First, I obeyed Him, and then He was able to transform my mind to think like God. Overnight I became a creationist. Overnight I believed that Joshua spoke, and the sun stood still. Overnight I believed that a whale swallowed Jonah and spat him out alive three days and three nights later. If the Bible had said so, I was prepared to believe that Jonah could have swallowed the whale! It didn't matter what the Bible said and whether it seemed practical or impossible. If God said it, it was true. I came to trust the Scripture by stepping out on every word as the inerrant truth of God.

That day I made a decision to change the way I read His Word. Instead of using my intellect as the primary tool, I would activate my spirit to listen to His Spirit. In this way He can communicate revelation to me which is sometimes a mystery and beyond the limitation of words. This is the wisdom He promised in First Corinthians 2:6-16.

I then made a threefold commitment to

1. Believe every word of Scripture like a little child even if I didn't understand it.

2. Obey every command of Scripture.

3. Claim every promise of Scripture for myself personally.

At the time, it was a "blind" step of obedience. Now, looking back, I have many years of experience to prove that God is not just as good as His Word; He's much better than His Word. I've become more and more convinced of the power and wonder of the written Word of God. I've seen many of the miracles recorded in the Bible with my own eyes. I've seen God's hand upon my life in the most incredible and wonderful ways, and it all began when I decided to trust His Word like a little child and live by these three principles.

UNBELIEF OF JESUS' DISCIPLES

Before we can fight the good fight of faith, we have to deal with this major obstacle of unbelief. Many Christians do not recognize the chronic unbelief in their hearts that cripples them and makes them powerless to move in faith. We need to understand how it got there and how to get rid of it.

Mark's Gospel, written around A.D. 50, was one of the first parts of the New Testament. False teachings were already present in the Church within the first twenty years. Shortly after the completion of Mark's Gospel, certain heretics in the Church began to attack and discredit it, particularly its ending. Some of the handwritten copies of Mark's Gospel were altered to omit the last few verses because some people thought they were not really Scripture. Even today, some theological circles question their authenticity, and some Bibles have a footnote: "The most reliable early manuscripts...do not have Mark 16:9–20." I do not want to debate these arguments of current scholarship here, but I can assure you that *the end of Mark's Gospel is absolutely trustworthy*. It is the Word of God.

What I want to show you is why this portion of Scripture came under such violent attack and why it is important for us to retain and proclaim this portion of Scripture. Some people want us to believe that Mark's Gospel finished at Mark 16 which says,

> *Trembling and bewildered, the women went out and fled from the tomb. They said nothing to anyone, because they were afraid* (Mark 16:8 NIV).

If the Gospel of Mark stopped here, we would be left without the certainty, power, and full glory of Jesus' resurrection.

In Mel Gibson's great movie, *The Passion of the Christ*, we are greatly impacted by the agony and pain of the cross, but we are not adequately impacted with the glory of the resurrection. Of course, we must appreciate the great price Jesus paid atoning for our sins, but the Gospel story must end with the glory of the resurrection, not with His suffering on the cross.

If we only believe in a Jesus who died for us, we have missed the power of the resurrection. On many religious crosses, Jesus still hangs as a tormented, pathetic figure, and the devil tries to keep Him that way in the minds of many Christians. That was a brief, temporary humiliation in order to achieve a much more glorious eternal purpose, and it's now over; it is finished! He is the risen Lord, the Conqueror, the Mighty God, the Ruler of Heaven and Earth, the King of kings, the Lord of lords, and the Highly Exalted One seated upon His throne!

The verses which are disputed begin at Mark 16:

*When Jesus rose early on the first day of the week, He appeared first to Mary Magdalene, out of whom He had driven seven demons. She went and told those who had been with Him and who were mourning and weeping. When they heard that Jesus was alive and that she had seen Him, **they did not believe it** (Mark 16:9-11 NIV).*

The disciples were weeping and mourning and did not believe Mary Magdalene's excited report that she had seen Jesus alive. Verse 12 continues,

After that, He appeared in another form to two of them as they walked and went into the country. And they

*went and told it to the rest; **but they did not believe them either*** (Mark 16:12-13 NIV).

UNBELIEF IS A SPIRIT

I want you to see the unbelief that is being emphasized in these verses. Unbelief, as opposed to an absence of faith, is not natural or reasonable; it is a spirit that comes from the devil. It works the same way as faith but in totally the opposite direction.

When we have unbelief in our heart, we will not believe even when reasonable, natural evidence is presented to us. Why did they think that Mary Magdalene had suddenly become a liar? Why would they think that these two disciples were declaring, "He has appeared to us!" if it had not actually happened? When confronted by at least three people testifying that they had seen Jesus alive after His resurrection, the disciples still said, "We don't believe you."

These were not the kind of people who told lies. They were people who told the truth, so it was not reasonable for the disciples to react in this unbelieving manner. The facts should have been enough for them to believe, but they could not be convinced because a spirit was at work in their hearts and minds. The absence of faith is bad, but unbelief is much worse because it blocks the spirit of faith that comes from God. You either have one spirit or the other. You cannot have both. Many Christians are unaware that they are still full of unbelief.

The disciples were Christian unbelievers. They walked with Jesus for three-and-a-half years and saw Him perform many miracles. They saw Him raise Lazarus from the dead, but unbelief still stopped them from believing in the resurrection of the Lord.

Remember, unbelief is not simply the absence of faith; it is worse than that. It is an active resistance against believing and is generated by an evil spirit controlling our human spirit. As a result, we choose not to believe, even when the physical evidence should convince us. It works like faith but in totally the opposite direction.

HATE UNBELIEF LIKE GOD HATES IT

Ever since God showed me the unbelief in my heart, I have waged war against unbelief and have come to hate it like God hates it. I would rather step out in reckless faith and end up looking stupid than be bound with a cautious spirit of fear and unbelief and miss the possibility of God doing a miracle. I have seen some wonderful miracles, but I also have had some spectacular failures.

At a big convention of eight thousand people, I prayed for a man in a wheelchair. I was sure God was going to heal him, but nothing happened. Embarrassed, I said to myself that I would never do that again. However, I could not live that way because I knew I was born for miracles (see Isa. 8:18). I just had to keep trying, making mistakes, and learning. Today I have learned a lot more about the ways of faith, but I still have a long way to go to become like Jesus, who never failed, but always healed them all.

Unbelief must be removed from your heart so that you become a person of faith and are not filled with doubt and unbelief. You need to hate unbelief the way God hates it and come violently against it. In Matthew 16:13, Jesus asked

Peter and the others, "Who do men say that I am?" They gave various opinions.

Jesus pressed them:

"But what about you?" He asked, "Who do you say I am?" Simon Peter answered, "You are the Christ, the Son of the living God." Jesus replied, "Blessed are you, Simon son of Jonah, for this was not revealed to you by man, but by My Father in heaven" (Matthew 16:15-17 NIV).

Jesus pressed His disciples because He knew they needed more than just teaching for their minds. They needed supernatural revelation from God to enable their spirits to understand. When Jesus heard Peter's declaration, which came from God, He promised, *"I will build a church out of people like you, Peter. You are receiving revelation from God's Spirit about who I am. The gates of hell cannot stand against such a church. I will give you authority to bind or loose on earth anything you want"* (see Matt. 16:17-19).

Now notice verse 21:

*From that time on Jesus began to explain to His disciples that He must go to Jerusalem and suffer many things at the hands of the elders, chief priests and teachers of the law, and that **He must be killed and on the third day be raised to life*** (Matthew 16:21).

Jesus had never lied to them, so it was reasonable for them to believe what He said. He clearly told them, "Listen men, this is what is going to happen. This is the purpose of My coming. It is all in God's plan. This is the power by which I will build my Church. My *mind-to-mind* teaching will not do it. We must go beyond that to something in the spirit realm. *Spirit-to spirit* I will show you the power of the resurrection. I must die for the purpose of defeating every demon and destroying every power." By His amazing faith, Jesus was able to look beyond the few hours of terrible suffering on the cross to the total eternal triumph and victory that He would obtain through His resurrection. Through His obedience, His Father would highly exalt Him and give Him all power and authority in Heaven and on Earth and under the Earth (see Phil. 2:5-11). Therefore He could even look at the cross with joy (see Heb. 12:2).

Peter protested at the idea of Jesus being killed: *"Far be it from You, Lord. I don't like this business about You dying."* When Peter spoke this way, Jesus rebuked him, "Get behind Me Satan!" (Matthew 16:23), showing that this unbelief is the work of satan. Peter had received revelation from God, but when it came to believing in the resurrection, he chose to listen to satan rather than Jesus.

ON THE THIRD DAY!

What Jesus spoke to His disciples about His death and resurrection is recorded no less than 17 times in the four Gospels, but they did not hear Him.

Just then there appeared before them Moses and Elijah, talking with Jesus. Peter said to Jesus, "Lord, it is good for us to be here. If you wish, I will put up three shelters—one for you, one for Moses and one for Elijah." While he was still speaking, a bright cloud enveloped them, and a voice from the cloud said, "This

is my Son, whom I love; with him I am well pleased.
Listen to him!"(Matthew 17:3–5 NIV).

If you read Luke's version, then you understand that the content of their conversation concerned Jesus' departure and His resurrection (see Luke 9:31). These disciples were having incredible supernatural revelation given to them, but they were too star-struck to pay attention to the revelation. At this point, the Father got involved in provoking the disciples to listen to what was being said. Peter was busy expressing his own ideas: "if you wish I'll put up shelters…" (see Matt. 17:4), but God interrupted him with a bright cloud saying, "*This is my Son….Listen to Him!*" (Matt. 17:5 NIV).

In Matthew 17:22–23, Jesus told them:

"The Son of Man is going to be betrayed into the hands of men. They will kill him, and **on the third day he will be raised to life.**" *And the disciples were filled with grief.*

Jesus knew that He would be betrayed and then killed, but would be raised to life on the third day. The following verses say the same thing:

Matthew 12:40 NIV: "For as Jonah was *three days* and *three nights* in the belly of a huge fish, so the Son of Man will be three days and three nights in the heart of the earth."

Matthew 20:17-19 NIV: "Now as Jesus was going up to Jerusalem, He took the twelve disciples aside and said to them, 'We are going up to Jerusalem, and the Son of Man will be betrayed to the chief priests and the teachers of the law. They will condemn Him to death and will turn Him over to the Gentiles to be mocked and flogged and crucified. *On the third day he will be raised to life!'"*

Matthew 27:61-64 NIV: "Mary Magdalene and the other Mary were sitting there opposite the tomb. The next day, the one after Preparation Day, the chief priests and the Pharisees went to Pilate. 'Sir,' they said, 'we remember that while He was still alive that deceiver said, *"After three days I will rise again."* So give the order for the tomb to be made secure until the *third day.* Otherwise, His disciples may come and steal the body and tell the people that He has been raised from the dead. This last deception will be worse than the first.'"

Mark 9:30-31 NIV: "They left that place and passed through Galilee. Jesus did not want anyone to know where they were, because He was teaching His disciples. He said to them, 'The Son of Man is going to be betrayed into the hands of men. They will kill Him, *and after three days He will rise.'"*

Mark 10:32-34 NIV: "Again He took the Twelve aside and told them what was going to happen to Him. 'We are going up to Jerusalem,' He said, 'and the Son of Man will be betrayed to the chief priests and teachers of the law. They will condemn Him to death and will hand Him over to the Gentiles, who will mock Him and spit on Him, flog Him and kill Him. *Three days later He will rise.'"*

Luke 9:22 NIV: "And He said, "The Son of Man must suffer many things and be rejected by the elders, chief priests and teachers of the law, and He must be killed and *on the third day be raised to life."*

Luke 18:31-33 NIV: "Jesus took the twelve aside and told them, "We are going up to Jerusalem, and everything that is written by the prophets about the Son of Man will be fulfilled. He will be handed over to the Gentiles. They will mock Him, insult Him, spit on Him, flog Him and kill Him. *On the third day He will rise again.*"

John 2:18-22 NIV: "Then the Jews demanded of Him, 'What miraculous sign can you show us to prove your authority to do all this?' Jesus answered them, 'Destroy this temple, and *I will raise it again in three days.'* The Jews replied, 'It has taken forty-six years to build this temple, and you are going to raise it in three days?' But the temple He had spoken of was His body. After He was raised from the dead, His disciples recalled what He had said."

If Jesus said something once, you would probably believe it. If He told you the same thing 17 times, surely you would believe it! Jesus understood that His disciples had a problem believing this, which is why He said it so plainly and so often.

The Gospel of Mark mentions the two men on the road to Emmaus, but Luke gives more details about this encounter.

Now that same day, two of them were going to a village called Emmaus, about seven miles from Jerusalem. They were talking with each other about everything that had happened. As they talked and discussed these things with each other, Jesus Himself came up and walked along with them; but they were kept from recognizing Him. He asked them, "What are you discussing together as you walk along?" They stood still, their faces downcast. One of them, named Cleopas, asked Him, "Are you only a visitor to Jerusalem and do not know the things that have happened there in these days?" "What things?" He asked (Luke 24:13-19 NIV).

These men did not recognize Jesus, and it is amazing that they talked about Jesus in the past tense, *"About Jesus of Nazareth, He was a prophet, powerful in word and deed before God and all the people"* (Luke 24:19). It is even more astonishing that they then began to repeat word for word what Jesus had said 17 times, *"The chief priests and our rulers handed him over to be sentenced to death, and they crucified Him"* (Luke 24:20). They told Jesus what He had said to them, but somehow nothing had registered in their hearts.

Verse 21 says, "But we *had hoped* that He was the one who was going to redeem Israel" (Luke 24:21). Notice again the past tense. And then comes the most amazing statement, "And what is more, *it is the third day* since all this took place" (Luke 24:21). These men had taken in everything Jesus had said but had been unable to believe Him. Despite all His teaching, preaching, and private conversations, everyone was still walking around in unbelief. The disciples should have been at the tomb waiting for Him to come out saying, "I want to be the first one to see Him rise!" That would have been the reasonable thing to do.

A spirit of unbelief had a hold on them, and they believed satan's lie rather than the truth. The disciples were crying and mourning in defeat and discouragement. All their hopes and dreams had been dashed to the ground, and everyone talked in the past tense, *"We had hoped... We thought... We once believed... but not anymore. It is all over."*

The story continues:

In addition, some of our women amazed us. They went to the tomb early this morning but didn't find His body. They came and told us that they had seen a vision of angels, who said He was alive (Luke 24:22–23 NIV).

These men ignored the evidence and walked with grief on the road to Emmaus rather than believe the women's story about angels. They also added:

Then some of our companions went to the tomb and found it just as the women had said, but Him they did not see (Luke 24:24 NIV).

They had an empty tomb. They had testifying angels. A company of people had testified that He was not in the tomb, but they still did not believe. Finally, Jesus entered the conversation in verse 25:

*"**How foolish you are**, and **how slow of heart to believe** all that the prophets have spoken! Did not the Christ have to suffer these things and then enter His glory?" And beginning with Moses and all the Prophets, He explained to them what was said in all the Scriptures concerning Himself. As they approached the village to which they were going, Jesus acted as if He were going farther. But they urged Him strongly, "Stay with us, for it is nearly evening; the day is almost over." So He went in to stay with them. When He was at the table with them, He took bread, gave thanks, broke it and began to give it to them. Then their eyes were opened and they recognized Him, and He disappeared from their sight* (Luke 24:25–31 NIV).

Looking at how many times Jesus had told them what was going to happen, and their determination to disbelieve everyone who testified that He had risen, it is easy to understand that Jesus' rebuke was justified.

> *They asked each other, "Were not our hearts burning within us while He talked with us on the road and opened the Scriptures to us?" They got up and returned at once to Jerusalem. There they found the Eleven and those with them, assembled together and saying, "It is true! The Lord has risen and has appeared to Simon." Then the two told what had happened on the way, and how Jesus was recognized by them when He broke the bread. While they were still talking about this, Jesus Himself stood among them and said to them, "Peace be with you." They were startled and frightened, thinking they saw a ghost* (Luke 24:32-37 NIV).

Many Christians tend to attribute anything supernatural to the devil. When Jesus came walking on the water, the disciples were afraid and cried out, *"It's a ghost"* (see Matt. 14:26). In other words, *"It's a demon."* Many Christians are quick to believe in a supernatural devil but have difficulty believing in a supernatural Christ.

Jesus continued in Luke 24:

> *"Why are you troubled, and **why do doubts rise in your minds?** Look at My hands and My feet. It is I Myself! Touch Me and see; a ghost does not have flesh and bones, as you see I have." When He had said this, He showed them His hands and feet* (Luke 24:38-40 NIV).

Jesus addressed the doubts that were still occupying their minds, but something was terribly wrong with the disciples' ability to believe. Despite all the evidence, including the Lord Himself standing before them, they still could not believe. Verse 41 is the climax:

> **And while they still did not believe it** because of joy and amazement, He asked them, "Do you have anything here to eat?" They gave Him a piece of broiled fish, and He took it and ate it in their presence. He said to them, "This is what I told you while I was still with you: Everything must be fulfilled that is written about Me in the Law of Moses, the Prophets and the Psalms." Then He opened their minds so they could understand the Scriptures. He told them, "This is what is written: The Christ will suffer and rise from the dead on the third day, and repentance and forgiveness of sins will be preached in His name to all nations, beginning at Jerusalem. You are witnesses of these things. I am going to send you what My Father has promised; but stay in the city until you have been clothed with power from on high." When He had led them out to the vicinity of Bethany, He lifted up His hands and blessed them. While He was blessing them, He left them and was taken up into heaven. Then they worshiped Him and returned to Jerusalem with great joy. And they stayed continually at the temple, praising God (Luke 24:41-53 NIV).

Until Jesus dealt with the unbelief in His disciples, they could not receive the faith that would empower them to advance the Kingdom in power. He strongly rebuked them for their unbelief and brought them to repentance. Like the disciples, you must get out of unbelief and into faith. I hope you will be honest with God as you pray.

God, if there is unbelief in me, get it out. I know I am receiving revelation from God, yet I am still captured by the devil. I want this devilish way of thinking to be cast out of me. I want to hate unbelief the way You hate it. I ask You to deliver me. Release me from unbelief that I might be filled with the true faith of God. May I be empowered to do exploits in Your name.

Just like those first disciples, when this transformation has taken place, first in our hearts and lives, then we will see transformation in our cities. We want our cities to be transformed. They will not be transformed until we are transformed. Please do this miracle for the glory of Your mighty name. In Jesus' name! Amen!

CHAPTER 4

ACTING IN FAITH

One morning God told me to look at every verb having to do with prayer, every verb having to do with any kind of work or act of the miraculous, and every verb that resulted in people becoming faith-filled. He told me to look at what grammatical voice is used in those verbs. I found to my amazement that there is an almost 100 percent consistency.

Every verb that resulted in someone becoming a man or woman who could move in faith is in the passive voice. In order to be filled with faith, you must become the recipient of something that comes from outside of you into you. It is grammatically called the passive voice. However, as mentioned earlier the English word passive doesn't quite express the meaning of this voice. It means being an active receiver. You have to be active in receiving faith. The source is outside of you, and you become the beneficiary or recipient of something given or imparted to you. It only really works if you are an active recipient of what is being given to you.

It is the nature of every human being to doubt. The only way for you as a human being to become a believer is to open up your spirit and for God to impart the very eternal life of God to you. The Holy Spirit pours the eternal life of

God into you, and in that life is the inherent ability to believe. By the power of that life, by laying hold of what God has given, comes the ability to believe.

Every verb regarding prayer is in the middle voice. The middle voice describes an action which is incomplete in itself. It requires a second separate action to complete the purpose of the first action.

To explain what this means, imagine that Frank and I are going to put up a tent. If I hold the tent peg for Frank so that he can drive it into the ground, you could say, "Alan is holding the tent peg." In Greek this would be written in the middle voice. The purpose of my holding the tent peg is for Frank to pound it into the ground. Together we achieve a purpose, but it requires action on the part of Frank to complete the purpose of my action. I could hold the tent peg all day long, but if Frank doesn't actively strike it into the ground, nothing is accomplished by my just holding it.

Almost every verb associated with prayer is in the middle voice. It does not accomplish anything if you don't add the action to the prayer. We must follow up our faith-filled prayers with action. Prayers of faith accomplish nothing if we do nothing except pray.

Every verb having to do with stepping out to work miracles or other works of faith is in the active voice. In the active voice, the subject of the sentence does something active to the object. If Frank raises his arm and strikes the tent peg, you might say, "Frank hits the tent peg." That would be written in the active voice. Faith requires action.

In Luke 5:16-17, Jesus prayed all night, and as a result, the power of the Lord was present to heal. The power of the Lord, which provided the possibility of miracles taking place, was produced by the mighty prayer life of Jesus. However, nothing happened just by His praying. Four friends of a lame man carried their friend into that atmosphere. They acted in faith and cashed in on the atmosphere that Jesus had produced by His prayers. If they hadn't walked in with their friend, nothing would have happened. No healing would have taken place until someone moved. You have to have the action of faith moving in the atmosphere where the power of the Lord is present. The action of faith is only fruitful when it moves in the atmosphere created by the right kind of prayer life. "Pray–ers" and workers have to work together. It can be the same person or different groups of people, but we need both. We need each other in order to see results.

You must lay hold of the eternal life of God until you are no longer living by your natural life but by the power of the risen life of God. Once you have received the faith of God, you must act as well as pray. You have to speak to the mountains, curse the fig trees, and give what you have been given. Every time individuals became men or women of faith in Scripture, it was because they became effectual recipients of what God gave them. Every time someone moved in the miraculous, it was because they added action to the atmosphere created by prayer.

Romans 12:1 instructs us to give Him our bodies as living sacrifices; Romans 12:2 says we should renew our minds to think like God. Then in verse 3, we are told to have a sober assessment of the measure of faith Christ has given us (see

Rom. 12:3). God gives each of us a measure of faith. However, it is not the same for everyone. God is a good investor; He will give faith where it is properly put to work. If you take your faith to the limit, then He will give you more. If you live well within the comfort zone of your present faith, then you will probably lose faith rather than gain faith. There is no way that someone can just lay hands on you and give you the fullness of God's faith. You will only get a measure of faith. What you do with that measure of faith determines how much more God is going to give you. Like muscles, faith only gets stronger by exercise. If it is not used, it wastes away.

Paul says we are to evaluate ourselves not by new techniques we've learned but by whether God has dealt to us greater measures of faith. After receiving faith, we must move quickly to use it for the purpose for which it was given. Prayers of faith must be accompanied by acts of faith. You must believe that what you have within you is Almighty God. God says, "*If you love Me, if you keep My commandments and obey what I say, then the Father, the Son, and the Holy Spirit will come, and We will make Our residence in you. We will use your humanity the way We used the humanity of Jesus. We can do through your humanity whatever We did through His humanity*" (see John 14:15-21).

It is either true or not true that the triune God has come to live within you. Don't play games. If you have died to yourself, then He will come and live in you. If you are keeping your self-life alive, then there is no room for God to come and live in you at the same time.

After you have received such a gift of faith, the Lord will almost immediately present a situation where you must move in faith. James 2:26 tells us that "faith without works is dead" (James 2:26). This is because God gives faith to you in order to accomplish something. You must step out and use the faith that God has given you. Do not listen to reason or respond only to your eyes and other natural senses. Listen to God and step out in faith, obeying what He is saying in your heart. He will develop your faith, and you will become more and more faith-filled.

THE PROMISED LAND OR THE WHOLE WORLD?

As we step out in faith, God gives us more faith. As we move from faith to faith, our vision gets bigger. We cease to be content with small things and begin to expect the big things. God is Almighty God. He can do anything. He is looking for people who will take Him at His word and believe Him for those things that seem impossible. He is looking for the people who will claim the nations as their inheritance.

Look at Romans 4:13 again:

For the promise, that he should be the heir of the world, was not to Abraham, or to his seed, through the law, but through the righteousness of faith (KJV).

When Abraham left the Ur of the Chaldeans, he was traveling to a few thousand square miles of land that is present-day Israel, a tiny spot on the face of the Earth. But by the time God brought him there, Abraham realized that it was not what God was talking about. Hebrews 11:8-10 says that when Abraham came to the promised land, he dwelt there as a sojourner, as an alien dwelling in tents, because he knew he had not yet arrived to the fullness of all that God had promised him. God can get you to start out on something only to take you on to something else much bigger that you did not plan for. God was working on His servant, and by the time Abraham came to the promised land, he saw something that included the whole world as his inheritance.

The whole world belongs to Abraham and his seed. The seed came to manifestation in the person of Jesus Christ. When it went into the ground and died, it brought forth the one many-membered seed, the Church. What goes into the ground and dies brings forth after its kind. We are the seed of Abraham, which means we own everything. This is not satan's world. He was the prince of this world until the cross, but he was judged and dispossessed at the cross. The one corporate seed of Abraham are the heirs of the world, which we receive by faith. The gold and silver belong to God and are stored up for the righteous to use obediently to fulfill God's purpose. Start thinking this way: *The devil is a usurper. The gold and silver are not his. Jesus and I own this place.*

We must become aggressive about these things. It is time to start stripping the devil of his resources and redirecting them to where they can be properly used.

> *Nevertheless I tell you the truth. It is to your advantage that I go away; for if I do not go away, the Helper will not come to you; but if I depart, I will send Him to you. And when He has come, He will convict the world of sin, and of righteousness, and of judgment: of sin, because they do not believe in Me; of righteousness, because I go to My Father and you see Me no more; of judgment, because the ruler of this world is judged* (John 16:7–11).

Jesus said that when the Spirit comes to you then He will convict the world. In other words, the Spirit comes to the world through you. There is only one way to fill your city with God's glory, and that is through you. There is only one way the Spirit will manifest Himself, and that is through you. When He has come to you, He will convict the world of sin, righteousness, and judgment.

The judgment mentioned here is not the judgment at the end of the age, but the judgment described in verse 11 (see John 16:7-11). We become empowered to show the world that the ruler of this world has already been judged. Every time you have a confrontation with the devil, you must remember that he has already been judged. Your job is to show the world that fact through your life. You don't back off when the devil attacks; instead, you counterattack and make him run. James says, "Resist the devil and he will flee from you" (James 4:7), but you must first submit yourself to God. Don't fight the devil in your own strength, but in Christ. Then you are more than a match for him.

> *Therefore it is of faith that it might be according to grace, so that the promise* **might be sure to all the seed,** *not only to those who are of the law, but also to those who are of the faith of Abraham, who is the father of us all* (Romans 4:16).

The promise is to all the seed. If the promise was according to gift or ability, then some people would be in, and others would not make it. God has made a level playing field so that anyone can get in. Faith comes from God, and He gives faith to us liberally if we put it to work. All of us can become like Abraham in our faith because he is "the father of us all" (Rom. 4:16).

Abraham received faith as a free gift and then acted according to the faith that he had received. He added action to faith. Peter also received it as a free gift and then added action to faith. Look at Acts 3. Peter had been in the upper room, the Spirit had come, and he finally had what Jesus had promised him. Peter had the faith of God. When he came to the lame man at the gate called beautiful in Acts 3, Peter looked at him and said:

> "Silver and gold I do not have, but what I do have I give you: In the name of Jesus Christ of Nazareth, rise up and walk." And he took him by the right hand and lifted him up, and immediately his feet and ankle bones received strength (Acts 3:6-7).

This is how you do works of faith. First, you must have total confidence in what you have. Peter knew what he had. You must know and comprehend who lives in you. If you devalue who has come to reside in you, then you don't believe in the resources that are available to work through you. When you come to realize that you have Almighty God, the Creator of all things, residing in you, your whole perspective changes regarding what you have.

When Peter went to the house of Aeneas, he wasn't trying to get Aeneas healed; he was just letting Jesus use his humanity to continue His works (see Acts 9:32-35). There is a way of praying for people that is like a switch. By faith you actively give them what you have. I was once in a conference with a very well-known powerful healer. During the conference, he turned to one of his assistants who was also praying for the sick and said, "David, don't just pray for them. Give them something!"

In Acts 3:12-16, Peter makes it very clear that it was not his godliness or power that made the lame man whole, but faith. It is the faith that comes to us through Him. Peter was saying, *"I've learned to be a good receiver and then give away what I have received, and that is why that man is standing before you whole. I'm not the source of the faith. It has nothing to do with me, my godliness, or power. I'm just a receptor who passes on what I have received."*

Peter wrote his second epistle "to those who have obtained [or more accurately, received] like precious faith with us by the righteousness of our God and Savior Jesus Christ" (2 Peter 1:1). He was writing to those who have learned how to receive the same faith of God. In other words Peter was saying, "If you have learned how to receive the faith of God like I have, then what I am now about to write applies to you. If you don't have God's faith, then this doesn't apply to you." He continues,

> *Grace and peace be multiplied to you in the knowledge of God and of Jesus our Lord* (2 Peter 1:2).

The Greek word translated as "knowledge" here is *epignosis*. It is a stronger form of the word that is used to describe the intimate relationship that a man has with a woman in marriage. You come to know God more than you know your own wife or husband in a perfect marriage. It is more intimate than the intimacy in a great marriage. That is what we are being called to. That is how faith flows to you. Peter was a hardened, sunburned, rough fisherman who learned to come into this deep intimacy with God, and this deep intimacy with God poured faith into him. Peter received this faith as a free gift through intimacy and then put it to work. A good translation of what he says would be: *His divine power has already **given** to us everything necessary for life and godliness, **through the knowledge** of Him who has called us to His own glory and excellence* (see 2 Peter 1:3).

You get into this realm of the spirit, where everything you need for life and godliness already exists, by knowing Him. The key is intimacy. Intimacy that just wants to be blessed can be rather selfish. Intimacy that seeks to be empowered to meet the needs of the world really makes God happy. If you don't stay in active intimacy with God, then there is no flow of faith or power. If you want to act in faith, then be intimate. That is where the impartation of divine life pours into you so that you may be a channel for it to flow out and meet the needs of others.

Sometimes you feel the power go through you. Jesus felt power go through Him when the woman touched His garment. Sometimes you don't feel a thing. I'm always prepared to have a go. Sometimes I know that it is a done deal. Sometimes I'm just confessing the general principles of Scripture rather than having a direct revelation regarding that particular incidence. I'm still learning, but I'm eager to press even further into these things.

James 5:20 promises that the prayer of faith will turn a sinner from the error of his or her ways and "will save a soul from death and cover a multitude of sins" (James 5:20). Some of you may have unsaved relatives, and you may have been praying for them for years. But have you been praying for them with faith? Have you received the title deed for them?

My salvation demonstrated that the prayer of faith really can turn *a sinner from the error of his ways and cover a multitude of sins* (see James 5:20). If you start receiving real faith for your relatives, neighbors, or colleagues at work, you will be thrilled at how many will be saved. If you wail and moan, praying prayers of desperation without faith, you will not receive the answer. Galatians 3:7 says, "Therefore know that only those who are of faith are sons of Abraham" (Gal. 3:7).

You cannot be Abraham's heir without Abraham's faith. You cannot inherit what God has promised Abraham unless you have received His faith.

God promised Abraham concerning every community, every people group, and every identifiable "ethnos" group that He was going to bless them by turning them away from their iniquities. If people start getting faith for things and then acting in faith, God is released to fulfill His Word through their faith. If you have Abraham's faith, then you can inherit what God promised Abraham.

Galatians 3 describes this:

And the Scripture, foreseeing that God would justify the Gentiles by faith, preached the gospel to Abraham beforehand, saying, "In you all the nations [ethnos or people groups] shall be blessed." So then those who are of faith are blessed with believing Abraham (Galatians 3:8-9).

God says that He is going to save nations, cities, and people through faith. My question is: whose faith is He going to use to save them? They cannot have faith for themselves because they are not believers. Someone else has to have faith for them. If you will stand in the gap and come to faith for your country or your city and all its needs, then a transformation can take place.

You must come to faith and believe that God can get hold of the media. He can cleanse and purify the media so that they begin to be a channel for God's blessings to the nation. We can take hold of the public school system and say, "God, I am not just going to moan about the education system. Instead, I am going to come to faith that You will remove the godless, corrupt people, replace them with God-fearing people, and change the whole system until it glorifies You."

You might say, "I'm looking to God for a powerful move among children in this church. I'm going to target the children until the Holy Spirit visits them with wave after wave of His love." Or, "I'm going to target the ethnic communities in my city. I'm going to get hold of all the rich businessmen of this city because they are in as much bondage to material wealth as any drug addict. God is going to break into their lives by His power through my faith."

These are the kind of prayers we can pray. Through faith, God will hear and answer. God loves to answer faith-filled prayers. God has already spoken such things in the realm of the spirit, but they require faith to become manifested on the Earth. We must combine the right kind of prayer life with the action of faith. We must open our eyes to see the fullness of what God has promised us. He has promised us the nations as our inheritance!

FAITH AND HEALING

We have seen that faith reaches into the realm of the spirit, gets hold of what God has said, and brings it into our earthly time-space world. Only then is it manifested in physical form. It comes out of the realm of the spirit and becomes physically manifested.

First Peter tells us that Jesus

Himself bore our sins in His own body on the tree, that we, having died to sins, might live for righteousness—by whose stripes you were healed (1 Peter 2:24).

Healing is spoken of in the past tense. God dealt with our sicknesses 2000 years ago when Jesus bore all our sicknesses, diseases, and pains in His body on the cross. He paid for them all so that you and I can live free from sickness. He did the same thing with our sins. It is a finished deal. In the realm of the spirit there is complete physical healing for all, but it cannot be manifest in your body until faith lays hold of it. It came into created existence by the word of God, but it comes into physical manifestation by the activity of human faith.

There is a sovereign side to this. We cannot of ourselves just decide to speak things into existence; only God can do that. However, God provides faith in order that we might grab hold of what He has already spoken into our hearts. Then we can speak it into manifestation just as Jesus did. The more we learn about faith, the more we are able to possess these things.

And the prayer of faith will save [sozo] the sick, and the Lord will raise him up. And if he has committed sins, he will be forgiven (James 5:15).

Sometimes people cannot be healed until they deal with the sin that caused the sickness. There is a close connection between certain sins and certain physical conditions. Sometimes healing is prevented because of sin. Although this is not always the case, bitterness and arthritis have a close connection. However, this verse says that the prayer of faith *will* heal the sick. The Lord will raise them up (see James 5:15). It does not suggest any other alternative. God will do it.

It must be a prayer of faith, not just a prayer of sympathy. It cannot be a prayer of pleading desperation. It must be a prayer of faith in Jesus alone. You cannot pray to God as one of the many different options you are trying at the same time. The only reason the Bible gives for failure in prayer is unbelief. We cannot create faith, but God will give faith to those who are prepared to use it.

SPEAK TO THE MOUNTAIN

One of the actions of faith is speaking. In fact, speaking is probably the primary action of faith. The greatest act of faith was when God spoke everything into existence out of nothing. Every visible work of faith comes from speaking what needs to be manifested, healed, rebuked, or cast out into actual physical existence. You never find Jesus anywhere in the Bible just praying about things or praying for things. We often talk about praying for the sick, but Jesus never did that. He just spoke and told the sicknesses and the demons to go, and they immediately went.

Jesus frequently told His hearers that He did nothing of Himself, but the words He spoke and the works He did were simply the Father and the Spirit speaking and working through Him. Jesus had a life of deep intimacy with His

Father and just did and said what His Father told him to. If we will fulfill the conditions of loving Him and keeping His commandments, He calls us to live in exactly the same relationship with the Father and speak and act just as He did (see John 5:19,30; John 14:10-15; John15:14-16).

Jesus had a fantastic prayer life, and His prayer life was the preparation which enabled Him to just speak the word of faith when He actually confronted the situation. It is not enough to just pray about mountains. You have to come to the place where you tell them to move. You must come to that place in your prayers where you know that what you say will come to pass just as God is always confident that what He says will come to pass. This confidence comes from knowing that we are speaking His word according to His will (see 1 John 5:14-15).

SATAN IS TERRIFIED OF REAL FAITH

God's own faith brings about the manifestation of God's own word. It is all from God and all for God. However, it is God's faith working through a human agency that causes His word to be manifested upon the Earth. A human agency is always necessary to be the channel of God's faith.

Because God is perfectly righteous, there are certain things that He cannot do, not because He lacks the power, but because He cannot violate His righteousness. God has given this world into the rule of man, and in this dispensation He must limit Himself to work through the agency of man.

The Bible says,

The heaven, even the heavens, are the Lord's; But the earth He has given to the children of men (Psalms 115:16).

God has never changed His original purpose to give Adam and his descendants the authority to rule over the Earth. Adam disobeyed and rebelled against God, thus opening up his life to the control of satan and allowing satan to bring his kingdom of darkness upon this Earth (see Eph. 2:1-4). Most people are deceived into thinking that they are free and independent, and are having a good time pleasing themselves. They do not know that they are actually under the power and authority of satan.

Adam and Eve's rebellion opened the door for the devil to establish his kingdom upon the Earth. Satan could only work through the vehicle of men and women because the Earth is still their domain and responsibility. Therefore, satan temporarily had dominion on Earth because they gave it to him, and it will only continue as long as they continue to give it to him. The devil is dependent on humankind's blindness and inadvertent submission in order to retain his now illegal rule over any part of the Earth.

Years ago, I asked God why He did not just wipe the devil off the face of the Earth. I thought this would make getting people saved so much easier. He graciously explained to me how foolish such an idea was. God said, "*Of course, I could wipe the devil off the face of the Earth at any time. But remember this, because of My righteousness, I cannot judge the devil finally and eternally without judging humankind in the same way at the same time as they were an accessory to the crime. I love all men and women, and I don't want to judge any of them. I want to give them opportunity to repent. Then I can forgive them and bring them back as joyful voluntary subjects of My Kingdom.*"

For a period of time, God has chosen to tolerate the activity of satan upon the Earth so that men and women may continue to have an opportunity to repent and be saved. Once God brings this period of Adam's rule to a close, it will no longer be possible for humankind to be saved. For the sake of lost men and women, God puts up with the activity of satan, but He certainly does not like it!

However, even now, if a person cries out to Him, God can answer. If a man or woman lays hold of God's words through faith, He can release His power to fulfill His word through that individual. If we want to see the works of God in our life, God's faith must be working through our humanity. Even though God has given great prophetic words through His prophets, somebody still needs to pray with faith so that those words become manifested upon the Earth.

The prophet Daniel is one of the great examples of this principle in Scripture. Daniel had read the Scriptures where Jeremiah and Isaiah prophesied that after seventy years of judgment God would bring His people out of captivity in Babylon and restore them to their own land. Daniel prayed for this to come to pass for more than fifty years before anything visibly began to happen. Without Daniel's prayers, God would not have been able to fulfill His Word on the Earth.

When we begin to see this, we realize that it is vital to come to faith-filled praying. We are the vehicle that causes God's Word to be manifested upon the Earth through our prayers of faith. That is why we hear God crying out again and again in Scripture for a man. The Earth was covered in darkness and wickedness, so God looked for a man to stand in the gap and be the agency through whom His Word could be fulfilled on Earth. By praying the prayer of faith, Daniel released God's mighty angels to righteously intervene and drive the devil and his forces out. The spiritual battle was so intense that Daniel grew weary and almost gave up, so Gabriel was sent to strengthen him and urge him not to stop praying. His prayers were a vital factor in this conflict. This was not simply God's independent, sovereign intervention, but it was His power working through a human channel of faith. Only then can angelic hosts righteously intervene in the affairs of humankind's domain. (See Daniel 10.)

A human agency is necessary so that God can righteously destroy the works of the devil and at the same time keep the door of salvation open to men and women. For a nation to change, there must be a person or community who will pray for it. They must receive God's faith so that His Word can come to pass on the Earth. God has already spoken and done everything necessary through the cross to destroy the devil's works and end his dominion on Earth.

That is why satan is terrified of real faith. He cannot undo God's Word because God has already spoken it into existence in the spirit realm. His only hope is to try to neutralize the Word of God through the unbelief of humankind. If he can stop God's people from believing, the Word of God cannot be manifested, and the works of God cannot be done. This is why the devil continually attacks faith-filled believers and why it is a constant battle of faith.

From our perspective, God sometimes appears to be powerless. However, we must understand that this is not a result of any weakness on His part, but is a result of His perfect righteousness and the unbelief of His people. Unbelief is such a serious issue because it stops God from being manifested through His Word and destroying all the works of satan. Through the faith of Christians, every word of God can be established upon the Earth. Therefore, satan does everything he can to rob us of our faith and prevent God's Word from being fulfilled.

CHAPTER 5

FAITH FOR COMPENSATION AND RESTITUTION

Because God is righteous, satan is permitted to test us. He was even permitted to test God's own Son. As a man, Jesus only knew who He was in the same way that we know who we are, through faith in the Word of God and the witness of the Holy Spirit to His human spirit. Therefore, the devil was allowed to test Him. When the devil tried to undermine Jesus' faith in who He was by trick questions and insidious twisted statements, Jesus only had one reply, "It is written!" So the devil had to leave Him. Jesus immediately returned from the wilderness "in the power of the Spirit" and began His miraculous ministry (Luke 4:14-15).

God is absolutely righteous, and therefore, the devil has to be given the right to challenge the reality of a man's or woman's faith. If that faith is proved genuine, he or she will have the authority to cast out the devil and totally dispossess him. God has to allow Christians to be tested in order to prove their faith is genuine. It is not really God testing you, but it is the devil challenging the faith of God, which is now resident in a human being.

This is a dangerous game for satan to play because if you keep your faith right through the end of the test, the devil will then have to pay heavy compensation. As a result, you can strip him of all his treasures and destroy his works. But, if he can cause you to lose your faith, then he can neutralize the Word of God through you and continue to exercise his influence in the Earth. He will attack our money, our health, our material possessions, and our relationships. He will try to put wedges between husbands and wives. He will try to alienate children from parents and brothers from sisters. He will attempt to produce moral failure, split churches, and divide leadership teams causing hurt and disappointment. His goal is to produce unbelief so that every human agency is rendered powerless by that unbelief.

CLAIMING COMPENSATION BY FAITH

The devil is a thief and a robber (see John 10:1), so we should not be surprised that he tries to rob us. God sometimes permits the devil to rob us. When this happens, we must keep our faith and learn how to claim compensation through the laws of restitution.

Everything in the Old Testament was written for our instruction. First Corinthians confirms this:

Now all these things happened to them as examples, and they were written for our admonition, upon whom the ends of the ages have come. Therefore let him who thinks he stands take heed lest he fall (1 Corinthians 10:11-12).

The Old Testament illustrates principles that apply even more in the New Testament, especially to those who live at the end of the age. Jesus said that not one jot or tittle from the law would be removed (see Matt. 5:18). The teaching of the New Testament exceeds the law in every way. We are certainly not bound by the legality or ceremony of the Old Testament, but the principles of the Old Testament are eternal truths that show us the heart and nature of God. A principle in the Old Testament becomes more powerfully true in the New Testament.

THIEVES HAVE TO PAY

One of the principles found in the Old Testament is that thieves have to pay! Exodus 22:1 is God's regulation for thieves:

> *If a man steals an ox or a sheep, and slaughters it or sells it, he shall restore five oxen for an ox and four sheep for a sheep* (Exodus 22:1).

To understand what an ox is in New Testament terms, we have to learn to read the Bible allegorically. Look at First Corinthians 9: "Who ever goes to war at his own expense? Who plants a vineyard and does not eat of its fruit? Or who tends a flock and does not drink of the milk of the flock? Do I say these things as a mere man? Or does not the law say the same also?" (1 Cor. 9:7-8). Paul is saying here that the authority of the law has something to say on these matters. Then he continues in verses 9-11:

> *For it is written in the law of Moses, "You shall not muzzle an ox while it treads out the grain." Is it oxen God is concerned about? Or does He say it altogether for our sakes? For our sakes, no doubt, this is written, that he who plows should plow in hope, and he who threshes in hope should be partaker of his hope. If we*

have sown spiritual things for you, is it a great thing if we reap your material things? (1 Corinthians 9:9-11).

Paul is teaching that a person who labors in the ministry is entitled to reap the reward of his ministry. He is like the ox in the Old Testament which must not be muzzled because it is entitled to eat the grain it is treading out. God is not primarily concerned with oxen but with men and women who labor in preaching and teaching.

An "ox" is someone who is called to full-time ministry in the Word. An "ox" is an elder, pastor, apostle, teacher, or minister who gives himself or herself to serving God's people by giving them instruction and admonition in the Word of God.

First Timothy 5:17 goes on to say:

Let the elders who rule well be counted worthy of double honor, especially those who labor in the word and doctrine (1 Timothy 5:17).

The Greek literally says that the elder who rules well is "worthy of double pay." The word *honor* means "the financial value you place upon God's man or woman who teaches you." In the Latin version it says, "*worthy of double honorarium.*" Those who are teaching and preaching should be regarded as being worthy of double pay. Then in verse 18, Paul continues:

For the Scripture says, "You shall not muzzle an ox while it treads out the grain," and "The laborer is worthy of his wages" (1 Timothy 5:18).

This is a consistent teaching in the New Testament.

CLAIMING RESTITUTION

We now need to interpret Exodus 22 in the light of the New Testament. Satan comes and attacks a church. Imagine that the devil deceives a gifted minister in the church, and that minister then leaves the church and takes some people with him. A new church is started somewhere else in the city, but you have been robbed. This scenario happens too often all around the world.

If a ministry partner is robbed from you, it is easy to be heartbroken at the division and fall into doubt, discouragement, and despair. You must keep your faith, go to the heavenly court, and say, "Lord, I am claiming full compensation for this robbery!" For every stolen ox, you are allowed to claim five oxen in return. Therefore, go to court and say to the Lord who is the righteous judge, "The devil has ripped away a wonderful ministry, and we are claiming five in return in Jesus' name!"

If you start making the devil pay full compensation, then he will not be so keen to come and attack you anymore. You must press your case and stand firmly upon your rights to demand full restitution. Do not be on the defensive, but go on the offensive to make the devil pay for robbing you.

Sheep in the New Testament are believers. If the devil steals fifty sheep from you then you are entitled to a fourfold return. If 50 believers are lost, you can claim 200 back! If you get hold of this principle, your trials will take on a whole new character. You cannot stop the attacks, but if you keep your faith and claim restitution, you will end up richer than you were before the attack.

But remember, you must keep your faith and learn how to claim restitution in the spirit realm so that legal compensation is made. If you give up or concede the theft, then you will live in defeat, and the devil will reduce you to a pauper. He will enjoy stealing from you because he knows you will not claim restitution from him. In this case, not only has he robbed people from you, but even worse, he has robbed you of your faith.

Can you see how practical this is? I have lived this way for years now and have seen these things work. I am not writing you theory but practice. Exodus also adds,

> *If the theft is certainly found alive in his hand, whether it is an ox or donkey or sheep, he shall restore double* (Exodus 22:4).

If satan comes and harasses one of your people but is unable to snatch him or her away, you are entitled to claim twofold compensation for the harassment. In the end, instead of having one believer, you can have three. I have practiced these things in recent years, and I tell you it works!

I hope you are beginning to say, "Hey, this is not so bad. If the devil robs me, it is not the end of the story, providing I keep my faith and seek restitution." Your whole view of trials changes when you understand this truth. At the time, these trials are hard and painful, but you know that you are going to claim full compensation.

> *People do not despise a thief if he steals to satisfy himself when he is starving. Yet when he is found, he must restore sevenfold; he may have to give up all the substance of his house* (Proverbs 6:30-31).

If you handle money righteously and honor the principle of giving tithes and offerings, then the devil has no right to steal your finances. If he steals from you, you can claim sevenfold compensation. Ever since this was revealed to me, I have always claimed sevenfold in such situations.

Once I was helping Pastor John Babu to build a church building in India. We needed $30,000 to finish it, and I had been praying for it. I do not believe in sending out begging letters but prefer to pray and let God send the money. A lady in Scotland was attending one of my meetings. I had never spoken to her personally, but later she heard the Lord speak to her while praying, *"Send $10,000 to Alan Vincent."* She obeyed and sent me the money. Her check arrived two days later. I immediately knew what the money was for although my name, Alan Vincent, was written on the check. I could have bought a new car or done anything else with that money. It would not have been illegal before the law of the land, but I knew that God had sent that money for a specific reason, which was for John's building. To buy a car in this case would have been spiritually illegal.

If you want God to fulfill your prayers, you have to be absolutely righteous in your financial dealings with Him. It is not enough to satisfy the law of the land and the tax authorities. You have to satisfy God, and His standards are much higher.

The $10,000 came, and I sent it quickly to John Babu in India, but it was stolen inside the Indian banking system, which sometimes happened in those days. They needed that money quickly, and I was mad, so I threatened the devil. I do not usually address the devil, but I did on this occasion. I said, *"Devil, I know what the Scriptures say. If you do not send that money back immediately then you will have to pay sevenfold compensation for what you have stolen. Even if you release the money immediately, you must still pay twofold compensation for even attempting to steal from me. You take your pick: twofold right now or sevenfold later!"*

Within two days the thief had been caught, and the money was returned. Then just three or four days later, I received another check in the mail for $20,000! Hallelujah! If the devil had not stolen the $10,000, then we would have been short $20,000. In reality, the devil helped us finish the church building. I like that!

If I had not known the law of restitution, I would have been moaning and groaning full of unbelief. But, because I knew about this law, I could keep my faith and exercise my right to compensation. I ended up with the $30,000 that we needed to complete the building. This truth changes your attitude toward trials. You need to practice these principles because they work!

PAINFUL YET JOYFUL

The New Testament writers also understood this law. James 1:2 exhorts us, *Brethren, be delirious with delight when you are in all kinds of trouble!* (see Jam. 1:2). We could think, "What's the matter with this guy? But James was the first senior pastor of the first church in Jerusalem, and he was writing these practicalities out of his own pastoral experience. He says, *"Look, when you are in various trials, rejoice about it because you know certain things. If you do not know these things, your trials will obviously not be a cause for joy but for misery. If you know certain things, then these trials can actually become a delight."*

The first thing we have to know is that the testing of our faith produces endurance. The Greek word for endurance is hupomone which means "longterm, cheerful endurance." It is not enough to stick in there and grind your teeth in a time of trial. You have to be happy about it. *Count it all joy, be delirious with delight when you fall into various trials knowing that the trying of your faith works patient, cheerful, long-term endurance. Let that endurance, that patience, have its perfect work that you may be complete, lacking nothing* (see Jam. 1:2-4).

You start your trial having been robbed of what you had, but you end with the devil compensating you and paying you what you didn't have in the first place! You are much richer after the trial than you were before the trial. Job is a good example of this principle. Satan came at him with everything he had, but Job kept his faith. Once satan ran out of accusations, Job received double of everything he had before. Like Job, the most important requirement is that you keep your faith!

Imagine that I approach your neighbor with a hefty piece of timber and hit him over the head with all my strength: *Bang!* A big bump appears on his head, and he shouts, "Oh, Hallelujah!" You would think, *This guy is crazy!* His head is throbbing with pain, and the bulge is protruding out of his head, but he is just smiling away saying, "Hallelujah!"

Imagine that this man knows something you do not know. He knows that every time I hit him over the head, I have to put $20,000 in his bank account. Therefore, every time I hit him, he begins rejoicing, "$40,000 now!" "Yes! $60,000 now!"

He endures the painful trial because he knows that his compensation is accumulating. It does not take away the pain, but a person can endure an amazing amount of suffering when he knows there is a great reward awaiting him at the end of the trial.

If you know the devil has to pay compensation when he attacks, you can endure the miserable feeling in your soul or body. In the end, satan has to pay for all the trouble he is causing you. There is a smile on your face, even while it is hurting, because you know that he has to pay back everything with interest. You will end up with more after the trial than you had before it happened. That is why you will be complete and lacking nothing.

Peter had the same revelation as James, as he wrote:

In this you greatly rejoice, though now for a little while,
if need be, you have been grieved by various trials
(1 Peter 1:6).

Peter understood that his readers had been grieved by painful events, but he also knew that they could still rejoice because there was no doubt about the ultimate outcome. You can be in pain and yet joyful at the same time, provided you understand this law of restitution. You can say to the devil, "You are really going to pay for this. I wouldn't be in your shoes when God brings the final judgment on you. You will have to pay heavy compensation for what you have been doing to me. There is no ground for you to attack me. You have robbed me of the legitimate objects of my faith, and now you are going to pay heavily for stealing what was rightfully mine. I am rejoicing even though I am hurting. It is painful, but for the joy of the result, I will hang in there and endure!" Hebrews exhorts us:

> *...let us run with endurance the race that is set before us* (Hebrews 12:1).

The next verse tells us how Jesus, the author and perfector of our faith, ran His race with endurance:

> *...who for the joy that was set before Him endured the cross, despising the shame, and has sat down at the right hand of the throne of God* (Hebrews 12:2).

We need to understand that Jesus accomplished a number of wonderful things simultaneously at the cross. The one we are most familiar with is the fact that He paid the full redemption price for all our sins so we could go completely free.

To adequately cover all the different things Jesus accomplished by His suffering on the cross would take a whole book on its own. But to better understand His mighty battle of faith we need to comprehend that He was also paying the redemption price to reclaim from the devil Adam's lost inheritance of being the ruler and owner, under God, of the whole Earth.

This subject is covered by many wonderful Scriptures that trace out the theme of this glorious Kinsman Redeemer. They basically teach us that the whole Earth is finally the Lord's. They show us that when individuals got into debt, and as a result their inheritance was sold to another, then at the time it was sold, terms and conditions of redemption had to be written out. Any blood relative could go at any time and, provided they were able to pay the full redemption price, they could recover what their relative had lost. (See Leviticus 25:23-25, Ruth 2–3, Jeremiah 32:6-17, and Revelation 5:1-10.) On the cross, Jesus the man reclaimed the whole Earth back from the devil and paid full redemption price.

Beyond the cross, Jesus could see the multitude of believers who were going to be saved. He could see the devil losing control all over the world and the whole of the devil's kingdom being destroyed and smashed. Jesus endured the most terrible experience any man has ever endured. However, as the devil was venting his spite and fury on this innocent man, Jesus was actually qualifying for compensation that would rob satan of everything.

Every time the devil hit Him, Jesus said, *Thank you very much! I'll take the United States.* With the next hit, He said, *Thank you very much! I will now take India!* As the blows increased, so did the compensation, until finally on the cross, He cried out in triumph, "It's finished! There is nothing to pay!" *I'll take all the nations! All the peoples will be mine. The whole world is mine!* As he endured the incredible suffering and humiliation of the cross, instead of giving up in defeat, he said with full authority, *Father, give Me the nations as My inheritance as You have already promised.*

If satan knows you are beginning to use this principle, his attitude toward you changes because it gets too expensive for him to keep robbing you. Once you start making him pay compensation, the attacks upon your life will reduce considerably.

Think of a man who walks down a New York street on his way to work. Every day he gets mugged. He doesn't resist or fight back, but just meekly hands the thief his wallet. Each time he comes, the same thief mugs him thinking, *This guy is easy picking!* Finally, this man decides to learn karate. Not knowing this, the robber attacks him again. This time our man pins him to the ground, roughs him up a bit, and demands his money back. From then on, the robber avoids him saying, "I won't touch that man again. It is too painful!"

If we meekly let satan rob us all the time, he will keep on robbing us. If we make a fight of it through faith, if we file a legal claim of compensation and enforce the judgment, he will say, "I am not going to touch that person anymore because it is too expensive." You will find that the attacks upon your life decrease because of the high cost of attacking you. However, if you just let him attack you without any resistance or response, then he will make your life a misery. If we keep our faith, we have the right to full compensation and the fun of making the devil pay!

FAITH AND THE OBJECTS OF FAITH

An important lesson we have to learn is that we must keep our faith even if we lose the object of our faith. There are times when God even allows the devil to rob us of the object of our faith. This can be very painful and is the most serious test of faith. However, we must always distinguish between faith itself and the object of our faith. If we are determined to be people of faith, then we must pass this test of faith, which occurs when the object that we are sure God has already given to us, is suddenly or tragically taken from us by the great thief satan.

To illustrate this, imagine that you have decided to buy a nice piece of land with a beautiful house on it. You have saved up a large amount of money and are intending to pay cash for the house. The owner has already agreed to sell it to you, but just as you are about to complete the contract, he changes his mind, reneges on his agreement with you, and sells it to someone else. You are bitterly disappointed. You have lost the object for which you have been saving for a long time. You are emotionally distraught from the pain of losing the fulfillment of your hopes and dreams.

Imagine that in your deep disappointment you go to the bank and withdraw all your money. You then take that pile of banknotes, the whole amount you have saved, and lay it out on the floor saying to yourself, *If we cannot buy the house we have saved all this money for, we might as well burn the whole lot!* So you light a match and set fire to the whole pile of notes. Within a few minutes, everything you had worked so hard for is gone.

You would be crazy to behave like that! Nevertheless, many people do just that spiritually. They pray for a long time over some issue and fight the good fight of faith, and they are almost there…. Then the devil is allowed to test them by stealing the object of their faith, and they just give up in deep disappointment and throw it all away. In defeat they mutter, "What a waste of time that was. All those hours of prayer for no purpose. What has it accomplished? Nothing!"

Listen to me! Do not lose your faith even if you lose the object of your faith. Although you lost the purpose of your prayers because of circumstances beyond your control, you are legally entitled to make the devil pay full compensation, which is at least double what you have lost. You must go to the heavenly court of Almighty God and demand your compensation. Insist that the devil has to pay according to the biblical principles by which thieves were required to make restitution for all they had stolen. The devil is a thief, and we must learn to make him pay and not let him just get away with it.

When you see and successfully practice these principles, it changes your whole attitude to trials. You can actually rejoice during the trial because you know the compensation that is coming.

SUMMARY

Both James and Peter understood these principles, practiced them, and taught them in their pastoral letters. As we have already said, James wrote,

> *Count it all joy* [literally be delirious with delight] *when you fall into various trials, knowing* [this] *that the trial of your faith produces* [endurance]. *Let patience have its perfect work* [so] *that you may* [become] *perfect and complete lacking nothing* (James 1:2-4).

Peter wrote,

> *In this you greatly rejoice, though now for a little while, if need be, you have been grieved by various trials, that the genuineness of your faith, being much more precious than gold that perishes, though it is tested by fire, may be found to praise, honor, and glory at the revelation of Jesus Christ* (1 Peter 1:6-7).

Remember the supreme example is Jesus Himself as He battled with the devil on the cross. By the time He was finished, He had taken everything from the devil and left him with nothing. Let us look to Jesus, the author and the completer of our faith, "who for the joy that was set before Him endured the cross, despising the shame and has sat down at the right hand of the throne of God," and let us copy His example (Heb. 12:2).

Also read Psalm 22:22–28 very carefully and see how Jesus claimed full compensation and stripped the devil of everything through His warring faith. If we let the devil rob us and get away with it every time, then he will go on attacking us unmercifully. We must learn to keep our faith and claim full compensation even when the object of our faith is stolen.

FAITH MUST LEARN TO PERSIST

There are two qualifications for this kind of compensation to be awarded you. You must first keep your faith. Secondly, you must learn to go to God's righteous courts in the heavenly realm, plead your case, and fight the legal battles necessary to obtain your compensation. Do not say, "That was a waste of time praying for that place!" Instead, keep your faith. Go to court claiming full compensation, and you will end up with much more purchasing power than you had before. Properly handled, the loss makes you richer not poorer. If you keep your faith, you will end up in a much better situation.

When you try to reach out in faith to obtain property for yourself or for God's work, when you try to get people healed, saved, or financially blessed, you will sometimes be disappointed because the object of your faith, which God had clearly told you was yours, is suddenly taken from you. This is the most severe test. If you keep your faith, you will receive something far better than the original object of your faith which you have lost.

If you lose your faith during this test, then you will lose everything, and satan will win in every way. He will have taken you out of the fight, and you will no longer be dangerous to him. To become a warrior in the good fight of faith, you will have to learn how to go before our righteous Judge, how to fight and win these legal battles. When you learn to fight these battles successfully, fighting the good fight of faith becomes real fun, and you end up richer and wiser than you were before. If you never learn this, then it ceases to be a good fight of faith and instead becomes a real misery of defeat and failure, because you lose so much and do not receive compensation.

Jesus gives us two parables in Luke that illustrate the need for persistence. We must take our case to the Judge and endure the trial. There is a process that we have to go through in order to receive what is legally ours.

Then He spoke a parable to them, that men always ought to pray and not lose heart, saying: "There was in a certain city a judge who did not fear God nor regard man. Now there was a widow in that city; and she came to him, saying, 'Get justice for me from my adversary.' And he would not for a while; but afterward he said within himself, 'Though I do not fear God nor regard man, yet because this widow troubles me I will

avenge her, lest by her continual coming she weary me'"
(Luke 18:1-5).

There was a widow woman in that city. She came in saying, "Give me *justice*" (see Luke 18:3). I think a better translation would be "avenge me" or "give me my legal rights." The word that comes four times in Luke 18:1-8 is *ekdikeō*, which is "that which proceeds from justice." She was saying, "I want my legal rights. What I am asking you for is legally my right, and I want it. Give me my legal rights over my adversary. Get justice for me."

Then the Lord said, "Hear what the unjust judge said. And shall God not avenge His own elect who cry out day and night to Him, though He bears long with them?" (Luke 18:6-7).

That word "bears long with them" is the Greek word *makrothumeō*. It means, "to have long-term, persistent passion about something." That is God's attitude about it. He cannot immediately act because He has to fulfill some legal requirements. He is not indifferent or lacking the desire or compassion. He is passionate about making the devil pay. He just does not have the legal right to move yet. He is bearing with them. It is not passivity; it is long term, persistent, passionate patience. He is saying, *"Just keep going! Keep going! Don't stop! As soon as I legally can, I will joyfully give you the verdict!"*

From a human point of view, it seems like you are praying to a God who doesn't care or who cannot help you, but that simply is not the case. He waits with persistent, passionate patience longing to answer you and send angels on your behalf. He is saying, *"Please don't give up the case! I want to send My angels, I want to answer you, but you have to complete the legal process. Please don't give up, because if you give up the case, My power to intervene righteously has gone. I have to work through the prayers of a man or woman."*

A woman in Jewish culture was despised, and a widow woman was not regarded as having any worth. She was pathetic, weak, trampled on, and worthless. Yet Jesus said, "If even one widow woman comes and pleads the case, then the righteous judge will give her the petition and avenge her of her adversaries" (see Luke 18:6-8). You don't have to be some great shining star in the Kingdom of God to win your legal battles against the devil; you just have to have persistent faith.

It does not matter if you are just one weak little widow woman with no money and no influence. If you know how to pray, that is enough. God has to give the devil every opportunity to bring his case against you. You have to go through the process, but in the end, He will legally give you what is yours. Jesus concluded by saying,

> *I tell you that He will avenge them speedily. Nevertheless, when the Son of Man comes, will He really find faith on the earth?"* (Luke 18:8).

Jesus is talking about the kind of faith that will not let go. He is not interested in how many suits you have. He is not looking at how many books you have written, how much time you have on television, or how many times your face has appeared on the front page of *Charisma*. When He comes, He will be looking for the kind of faith that lays hold of God's promises, faith that persists to the end, faith that sees the Kingdom of God powerfully manifested on Earth.

PERSISTING ON BEHALF OF OTHERS

As we fight the good fight of faith, our goal should be to get the kind of faith and pray the kind of prayers that can legally and righteously call down the resources of God to meet every need, not just for yourself but for everyone you come in contact with. In Luke 11:5 Jesus asks a question:

> *And He said to them, "Which of you shall have a friend, and go to him at midnight and say to him, 'Friend, lend me three loaves; for a friend of mine has come to me on his journey, and I have nothing to set before him'; and he will answer from within and say, 'Do not trouble me; the door is now shut, and my children are with me in bed; I cannot rise and give to you'? I say to you, though he will not rise and give to him because he is his friend, yet because of his persistence he will rise and give him as many as he needs* (Luke 11:5-8).

Notice that the triune God has to be your friend. We must spend time with God and have a genuine relationship with Him. The relational aspect is an important part of this parable. Intimacy is the key.

Notice what is being asked for. The three loaves are a picture of the triune God and the bread that came down from Heaven. The Father, Son, and Holy Spirit between them have everything that any human being could possibly need. Some people need the Spirit, some need the Father, and some need the Savior. We all need all of each of them, but the timing in which we receive them may vary according to our need. All the fullness of the triune God is seen in the three loaves.

Notice the reason you are asking. You have a friend in need, and you want something to set before him. We have the power to call down that bread, not just to satisfy ourselves, but to give it away to our friends in need. This kind of praying prays down the fullness of the Godhead into our being so that the fullness of the Godhead might be made available to meet the needs of anyone and everyone around us. If they need a Savior, I'll talk to them about Jesus. If they need the love of a father, then I'll talk to them about the Father. If they need the power of the Spirit to break some demonic curse off their life, then I'll talk to them about the Spirit.

You have a friend in need. We must stop living in an isolated Christian bubble where we have no friends in the world. We cannot continue to go to God only for ourselves. Our goal in the good fight of faith should not be just to come individually to faith but to come to corporate faith. Jesus was the friend of sinners, and we must live the same way.

America, like many other nations, is severely demonized in many ways and particularly in the area of broken families. Billions of dollars and thousands of social workers will not solve the problem. The families of America need Jesus and a revelation of the Father.

Social statistics tell us that 80 percent of the children in America are managing with only one biological parent. Some don't even have one of their original parents. Just imagine—80 percent! That means that only one child in five still lives with the two parents that gave birth to him or her. And sometimes even those families are dysfunctional. Individual faith is great, but we must broaden our vision. We must come to faith as a Body in order to impact the whole of society.

I want that widow woman's heart to cry out and persevere for the cities of the nations. I would rather have that than a personally successful ministry, a lovely home, or an abundance of this world's goods.

Often we plead in prayer but do not see immediate answers. It seems that God does not care, but that is not true at all! In these parables about persistent prayer, Jesus seems to characterize God as uncaring and indifferent; however, that is not the real truth. He says, "The Father will answer you right speedily," but you have to stick in there (see Luke 18:8).

In the natural, if you quit a "cast-iron" court case halfway through the hearing, you would lose the case because you did not persist to the end. The devil knows how to use every delaying tactic to discourage us and try to stave off the inevitable. Therefore, we have to stay in there, even if there is delay, because God has to do everything righteously. He is longing to give the verdict to us, but it has to be impeccably righteous because that is the nature of our God. So, He allows the devil to bring every contentious, lying argument before the court of Heaven. If we demonstrate a heart of persistent faith and stay the course, we will receive the verdict in the end.

A Grandmother Who "Prayed in Faith"

I was saved because of my praying grandmother. In my teens and twenties I rebelled against my Christian upbringing. I was working for the Kodak Film Company and called myself a scientific atheist. I was heading for a high position and was very ambitious.

My grandmother lived in my parents' home in England for a period during the last few years of her life. She was a wonderful praying old lady and looked with dismay at my total godlessness. Every Christmas she gave me a New Testament, and I am ashamed to say I threw each one away. I thought to myself, *I don't need that silly old book. She needs it because she's an old lady who is going to die soon. I don't need it.* Although she was half my size, a day came when she looked me in the eye, locked her eyes with mine, and said, "I've been praying, and God has promised me that one day Jesus is going to save you, and you are going to serve Him!" I laughed at such a preposterous idea.

My grandmother died without seeing her prayer answered on Earth. However, if you do not see the answer in this life, then you can still cash your "faith-checks" in Heaven where their purchasing power is automatically multiplied. I do not know what she did in Heaven when I got saved, but I imagine she probably danced a jig and said to Jesus, "Well, Lord, since I didn't get this prayer answered before I got to Heaven, I am going to ask for an increasing value. I don't just want him saved. I want him to be a terror to the devil!"

I was at the height of my success when I got saved. I was happily married, and I'd just landed a new job with a 60 percent increase in salary. We had just bought a fantastic new home and a wonderful new car. I didn't have any needs. At 28 I had arrived and was heading toward fame and fortune. In the middle of all that, God reached down from Heaven and said, "Now's the time to fulfill that promise." I couldn't have been more financially secure. I couldn't have been happier or more content. I was not in trouble, and I was not on drugs or alcohol. Nevertheless, God burst into my life and saved me in the most amazing way.

At the time, I was interested in immigrating to America to further my career, so I agreed to talk to two young Americans who turned out to be Mormon missionaries. They got me to read a book I didn't believe in, which was the Bible. I discovered that the Bible is powerful whether you believe in it or not. It's the sword of the Spirit of God. If I were to take a real sword and threaten to thrust it into someone, and he said, "Hey don't use that sword on me. I don't believe in swords!" it would not make any difference. It would still have the same penetrating effect. It is still powerful. These two Mormon missionaries got me to read the Bible, and I began to argue with them over what it really said. It didn't matter that I didn't believe the Bible at the time; it still convicted me.

After about three months, I was introduced to a local Christian who with a simple explanation of the Gospel led me to Christ. Eileen, my wife, followed me a few minutes later, and we were both saved the same night. The Mormons were furious when they learned we had been saved and said, "You've been sold that doctrine of salvation!" They tried hard to shake our newfound faith, but they couldn't do it. We had met God, and we knew it.

My granny died with real faith that I would be saved. She had obtained the title deed of my salvation. Like Abraham of old she "died in faith, not having received the promises" (Heb. 11:13). So she took her "faith check" with her to Heaven and cashed it there. She didn't give up simply because she didn't see the manifestation. She didn't lose her faith when I kept throwing away the Bibles she gave me. She persisted even into Heaven itself where her check was finally cashed with interest. She didn't just get her grandson passively saved, but, as compensation, got a faith-filled, devil-destroying warrior for a grandson!

LIVING AND DYING IN FAITH

The heroes of faith described in Hebrews 11 did not always see immediate answers to their faith. If I told you that living a faith-filled life was all push button easy, then I would be misleading you. My grandmother did not receive the answer to her prayers for my salvation until after she got to glory, but she did finally see it.

Perhaps the most severe test of faith is to die in faith—not just to die, but to die still trusting God without having seen the promise fulfilled. Hebrews 11 tells us about a whole series of heroes of faith:

Who through faith subdued kingdoms, worked righteousness, obtained promises, stopped the mouths of lions, quenched the violence of fire, escaped the edge of the sword, out of weakness were made strong, became valiant in battle, turned to flight the armies of the aliens. Women received their dead raised to life again... (Hebrews 11:33–35a).

But the tone changes in the middle of verse 35 where it says, "Others were tortured, not accepting deliverance, that they might obtain a better resurrection"; the subsequent verses go on to list many other terrible afflictions (Heb. 11:35b-38). Verse 39 explains,

And all these, having obtained a good testimony through faith, did not receive the promise (Hebrews 11:39).

I have heard some faith teachers say concerning someone who was not healed, "The reason this person died was because he didn't have enough faith." Sometimes that is not at all true. The Bible tells us that those who saw their prayers answered in this life were no more heroes of faith than those who died in faith without having seen the promise. In this life, they embraced them afar off as a "done deal" but never saw the fulfillment in this life.

When you know you have something by faith, you are not dependent on the material manifestation because you know it is already done. I have been through such tests. I was desperately sick when I went to India in 1963, and my doctor said I should stay near a hospital because I could need emergency treatment at any time. He was absolutely right. When I stepped onto the boat for India I thought God was going to heal me immediately because I had been obedient to Him. Instead, I went through another 12 years of terrible trials and nearly died several times. My wife Eileen also could tell you about the suffering she went through on my behalf. If she had not been a trained nurse, I probably would be dead. For seven years I kept asking and expecting God to heal me. Then through the writings of Smith Wigglesworth, I came to the place where I knew I was already healed in the spirit realm although there was no manifestation.

One morning God spoke to me and told me to anoint my nose with oil and just believe I was already healed. He said that He wanted to train me in the ways of faith, so He was going to allow the symptoms to continue even though I had already been healed. I was to testify that I had been healed and was not to pray anymore to be healed. Yet at the same time, I was to be honest and not to hide the fact that my nose was still bleeding. My mind was reeling under this apparent total contradiction, but understanding gradually came to my spirit. I walked this way for another five years, testifying that I had already been healed and yet still living with terrible, debilitating symptoms.

On several occasions I fainted as my lifeblood flowed out of my nose. Eileen had to stuff packing into my nose to stop me from bleeding to death. On those occasions, my life depended on her skill and speed to stop the bleeding. As things got worse, I became emaciated. My weight dropped to only about 130 pounds, and I had a very low hemoglobin count. I was a physical wreck. I also had asthma. If we had any baggage, Eileen had to carry it for me because I had no strength to carry it myself. I just staggered around. Frequently when I stood up to preach, I was so weak I did not know how I would manage to make it through.

Throughout that time, I knew I had a word from God that I had been healed, even though my physical condition continued to worsen. Some Hindu friends were very concerned for me and wanted to see me healed. One day they said to me, "Why don't you come and let our ayurvedic medicine people come and treat you? We're sure they could heal you. They have all kinds of wonderful powers. Your Jesus doesn't seem to be doing anything to help you."

The kind of medicine they were suggesting was a kind of homeopathy mixed up with the occult. I knew that their intentions were good, but the instrument was demonic. So I said to these dear friends, "I don't want to offend you, and I appreciate your love and concern. Although I cannot explain this, I want you to know that Jesus has already healed me. It's just not manifested, and I'd rather die believing in Jesus than be healed by the devil." Even if I had died, I would have died in faith.

God had rewired my scientific mind so that I could think this way. If I had died then, I would have died in faith, knowing that I had my healing although it was never manifested in this life. I cannot even explain that completely to myself, but I know it is spiritually true. I struggled under those terrible conditions, but I believe God allowed me to go through so much trouble for such a long time because He wanted to train me in the ways of faith. This is not theory. Everything I am teaching you, I have actually lived. In fact, I am still living this kind of faith to this present day.

When I made that statement to my Hindu friends, something happened in the spirit. A few days later all my symptoms disappeared, and I was visibly healed. I felt so much better and began to put on weight. My asthma disappeared, and I could feel a new energy surging through my body. I went to India in early 1963. I was healed in 1974; almost twelve years had passed. God did such a miracle for me that I now have more vitality than in my best years before I became a Christian. Now I am in my late seventies; I have plenty of energy, and I am much healthier than I was in my forties.

I could have died in faith without seeing any manifestation of my healing in this life. However, whether I lived or died, I would have still been a "hero of faith." I now understand how someone can die in faith without having received the promise, and God can still regard that person as a hero, equally powerful in faith as those who saw their deliverance in this life. The only difference is when and where the compensation for their faith was paid.

There are many stories of missionaries who died in faith, and then, years after their death, God poured out a mighty revival in the very place where they were working. In other words, the devil had to pay heavy compensation for killing them before they saw the manifestation of their faith. God didn't stop them from being killed, but He ensured adequate compensation for their faith.

Sometimes the manifestation of our faith is immediate. Other times it can be a long, protracted struggle. If you keep your faith, then you will receive full compensation for your faith either on Earth or in Heaven. If you can let go of your earthly, time-based perspective and develop an eternal perspective, then you will come to a point where it does not matter whether or not you see the manifestation during your life on Earth. You know the devil is going to pay sooner or later, and the longer he waits, the greater the compensation will be.

CHAPTER 6

JESUS, THE GREAT EXAMPLE OF FAITH

I n Paul's instructions to Timothy, he says,

*I urge you in the sight of God who gives life to all things, and **before Christ Jesus who witnessed the good confession before Pontius Pilate,** that you keep this commandment without spot, blameless until our Lord Jesus Christ's appearing* (1 Timothy 6:13-14).

I had never understood what this verse meant and why it was there until something very dramatic happened to me. In Britain, in the 1980s, I was leading one of the fastest growing churches in the country. We were seeing God bless us. He had given us the use of seventeen acres of land and buildings worth about $5 million for which we were only paying $7,000 a year in rent. It was a redundant senior high school, and the owners, who were the local council, had told us that we could buy it for a very low price after four years of paying rent.

We were set to have some of the best facilities in Great Britain. Already the property was being put to good use with a church, a wonderful Kingdom day school for 250 children, and an expanding network of churches. We were planning to begin a residential interns training program. It was a fantastic time with everything going for us. Then suddenly a property developer came and persuaded the local authorities to renege on their verbal promise; they quickly acted against our interests. The developer paid a large sum or money for this land, and we were given two weeks notice to move out.

It was as if a ferocious whirlwind suddenly enveloped us. We had to cancel all our plans. I was left high and dry with the church, the day school, and 250 nomadic children. People had sold their homes and bought houses to be close to our land. We had been certain that this was our Canaan, which God had given to us, and no one could take away from us. Suddenly it was gone, and I was absolutely devastated. The people were so hurt that they understandably vented their frustrations on me. I had never been in such a depressed state in all my life. I sat at my desk for about a year and could not preach on faith. I was devastated.

It was the sheer grace of God that kept me going. I was so deeply wounded that all the fire seemed to have gone out of me. But one day when I was reading this passage of Scripture, praying, and simply trying to stay alive, God spoke to me through this one phrase: *"Remember the good confession of Jesus Christ before Pontius Pilate!"* (see 1 Tim. 6:13-14). He showed me what it meant. He showed me how Jesus had fought such a good fight of faith during His trial and crucifixion—and particularly during His testimony before Pontius Pilate. I exploded into new life right there in my study. I danced, I shouted, and I got on my knees and repented for quitting the battle. That morning I got back into the fight and received a tremendous infusion of faith. By the grace of God, I am now a far greater threat to the devil than I was before that experience. In this chapter, I want to explain to you what God showed me that day.

The young, zealous Pharisee, Saul, was almost certainly an eyewitness to the good confession that Jesus made before Pontius Pilate. This experience was still vividly remembered by him when he became the apostle Paul, and it sustained him through more than thirty years of ministry. Paul told Timothy, *Remember what I told you about the good confession of Jesus Christ—and make sure you keep that same good confession* (see 1 Tim. 6:13-14).

A great mystery took place when God became man in the person of the Lord Jesus. From our perspective, it is easy to think of His divinity, but many people today cannot really imagine Him as being a true human being at the same time. Christianity has made Him into a sort of unreal superman, but that is not what He really was.

In the mystery of the incarnation, Almighty God, the Creator of all things, somehow shrank Himself into the limitations of one human person as Jesus of Nazareth. Jesus did not have the Adamic nature of sin, but He entered and lived for over 33 years in exactly the same humanity that Adam had in his innocence before he sinned. Jesus lived within the parameters of that human nature. He didn't function as Almighty God, but lived by the same powers and resources that are available to any man. He did not cease to be deity because He was fully and entirely Almighty God, but in His passion to save man, He did not once draw on the power of His own deity during the entire time that He lived as a man on Earth. God truly became man in order to make His Saviorhood righteous.

During His life on Earth, Jesus only knew who He was in the same way that you and I know who we are. For every moment of His human life, our Lord Jesus Christ lived as a man of faith. All He was and did flowed from the life of God within Him and the faith He had received from the Father. His humanity was constantly infused by the eternal life of God. That was the source of His faith. The only way Jesus knew His identity and what was available to Him came through revelation of the Word of God and the witness of the Spirit imparted to His human spirit. Jesus had no advantage over us once we have been born again. The way He lived by faith was the same way that you and I must live by faith. When you realize this and then look at His incredible prayer-life and all the things He accomplished in the same humanity as we have, you begin to worship and marvel at Him, not as some unattainable superman, but as one who shows us the way and literally invites us to imitate or mimic Him in every way.

GOOD CONFESSION OF CHRIST

We find Jesus' good confession was made during His trial preceding His crucifixion, the crunch point of His life of faith. Matthew records the first good confession of Jesus Christ when Caiaphas, the high priest said to Him:

> *I put you under oath by the living God: Tell us if you are the Christ, the Son of God!* (Matthew 26:63).

Jesus was tied up like a helpless prisoner, beaten, despised, and ridiculed. All His disciples had run away from Him. From a human viewpoint, Jesus looked like an utterly lost cause. His circumstances gave no indication that He was the Son of God with power. Nothing suggested that He was about to ascend to the throne of God and have all things come under His feet. Everything was screaming the exact opposite: *You are a failure!*

If Jesus had looked with His eyes, listened with His ears, or responded to the feelings of His soul, then He would have said, "This is completely crazy. I am a dead man! I am finished. The disciples have left Me. I am now in the power of these vicious political forces. They are going to destroy Me."

It was in those desperate circumstances they said to him, "Come on! Tell us now that you are a mighty king, you 'great god!' Look at yourself! You are just rubbish. You are living in complete religious hype. You are nobody. You are nothing. We can destroy you because we have all the power and all the authority. Look at your disciples! They have scattered and left you. And you are going to build a great Kingdom with them? Don't make us laugh. Tell us if you are the Christ, the Son of God!"

Jesus responded magnificently. He did not rely on His natural senses, but simply maintained His good confession of faith. Most English Bibles miss the full impact of what Jesus said. Perhaps the best way to translate His reply would be to use an Americanism that literally translates the force of the Greek. When Caiaphas said, "Are you the Christ, the Son of God?" Jesus replied, *You bet I am!*

That captures the Greek better. Not "thou hast said," nor "as you say." That's much too weak. Jesus said, "*You bet I am!*" It was the statement of fighting faith. There was the defiant, glorious faith of God Himself radiating from His eyes. He said to them, "You bet I am!"

Nevertheless, I say to you, hereafter you will see the Son of Man sitting at the right hand of the Power, and coming on the clouds of heaven (Matthew 26:64).

What a statement in that situation! But they did not apologize to Him or offer to release Him. Instead, they spat on Him and beat Him and dragged Him off to Pontius Pilate. If you make a good confession of faith, do not be surprised if the devil comes back at you with even greater fury to try to shake your faith. Your immediate circumstances may get worse and not better.

After Caiaphas, they then dragged Him before Pontius Pilate. Has anyone looked less like a king than the Lord Jesus did at that particular moment? His face was beaten to a pulp and covered in spittle. The blood running down His face was mixed with sweat. His back was striped and bleeding after the lashings of the Roman whip. His hands were tied, and a mocking crown of thorns sat upon His head. They did whatever they liked to Him. He was a toy in their hands. Yet a supernatural light shone from the eyes of that battered, bruised face (see Isa. 52:13-15; 53:3-10; John 19:1-22).

In John 18:33-37 Pilate enters the Praetorium and speaks to Jesus. He finally asks Him in verse 37: "Are you a king then?" Jesus immediately replies, "You bet I am! For this cause I was born and for this cause I came into the world."

That was a good confession! There is a strong tradition, which I personally believe, that Saul was a member of the Sanhedrin and was a spectator to these events. I am convinced that the Holy Spirit riveted those words deep into the heart of Saul the Pharisee as he actually heard that confident confession, "You bet I am!" and he never forgot that confession for the rest of his life.

Perhaps he thought, *That man is speaking the truth. That man has got a strange authority, even in his shameful circumstances. He should look defeated, but He is standing there like a glorious victor confessing an amazing good confession.* His words and His demeanor had a ring of truth and authority about them. Jesus' good confession had pricked Saul's heart.

When Pilate heard that good confession, with those eyes fixed on him, he also instinctively knew that Jesus spoke the truth. The circumstances totally contradicted His kingship, but His confession said, *I'm a king.* Pilate knew that Jesus was a righteous man. He knew that Jesus was who He said He was. However, Pilate did not have the courage to stand up boldly and agree with Him. Therefore, he just washed his hands and tried to politically extricate himself from the situation.

The crime of a convicted criminal was always written and fixed to the cross where he hung. When the time came to write Jesus' crime for the record books, Pilate had the sign written, "The King of the Jews" in Hebrew, Greek, and Latin. The religious leaders said to him, "Hey, don't say that. Write: 'He said he was the King of the Jews.'"

Pilate answered, "What I have written, I have written" (John 19:22).

He was essentially saying, *I know who this man is, but I don't have the guts to stand up for Him and His good confession.*

Before Jesus even went to the cross, He had fought a great battle of faith as He prayed in the Garden of Gethsemane and obtained the title deed of His resurrection. King David, who wrote Psalm 22 a thousand years before Jesus was crucified, must have been given an amazing vision of the cross. God must have shown David how Jesus claimed the nations and the Church as His inheritance. He could only have written that Psalm after vividly seeing Jesus in the utter blackness of Hell fighting the good fight of faith. Did Jesus say, *"Oh, poor old me. What a terrible situation I am experiencing"*? No! He didn't say that at all. Instead, He said, *Father, I'm claiming Your promise for the nations by faith.*

Jesus grabbed hold of God's promise to Abraham and to David and claimed the nations as His inheritance. He claimed a Church that would give itself completely to advance the Kingdom. The battle of faith He was fighting on the cross was the culmination of the most amazing fight of faith there has ever been.

JESUS THE GREAT WARRIOR OF FAITH

When I saw this for myself, I fell on my face and worshipped Him. I cried out, "Lord, You know all about faith! Jesus, in Your humanity You were the greatest warrior of faith there has ever been or the world has ever seen. I want to learn that from You." All the Kingdom advances which are happening in the world right now were obtained by faith when Jesus was on the cross. That is why there has to be a complete fulfillment of them all.

Paul must have heard Jesus Christ's good confession before Caiaphas the high priest and then before Pontius Pilate. He saw with his own eyes this amazing fighting man of faith. I believe the Lord revealed to him what Psalm 22 was all about. He saw how Jesus fought to take possession of all His inheritance, claiming all the promises by faith. In the most excruciating and unbelievably dark moments of the cross, Jesus did not give in to His circumstances, but triumphed over them through faith.

Some time later Saul was on the road to Damascus and was thrown from his high horse into the dust. A blazing light shone upon him from Heaven:

> Then he fell to the ground, and heard a voice saying to him, "Saul, Saul, why are you persecuting Me?" And he said, "Who are You, Lord?" Then the Lord said, "I am Jesus, whom you are persecuting. It is hard for you to kick against the goads" (Acts 9:4-5).

When Paul was finally saved and the Spirit of God began to instruct him, I am convinced the Spirit reminded him of Christ's good confession. Paul said, *I want to live like Jesus. I will always remember the good confession of Jesus Christ before Pontius Pilate and before Caiaphas. Timothy, you also must keep this command. Keep it blameless and spotless until the day of His appearing.*

That day as I saw how this convicting power had come upon Paul, I had a revelation of Jesus the man, fighting the good fight of faith. It simply broke me! I said, "*Oh God, forgive me for being such a wimp. Pour the Spirit of Christ into me. Let me be like Jesus. Let me fight the good fight of faith like Him.*" I got back into the battle and have been in it ever since.

This revelation transformed my life, and I trust it will do the same for you. However black the situation, it is not as black as the cross was for Jesus. There is a power in God's risen life to enable you to fight a good fight of faith and to obtain your inheritance while robbing the devil at the same time. You can have the title deed to your inheritance and overcome the evil one.

That is where God wants to bring us. Let these words sink into your heart right now. Maybe you feel the way I felt when God showed me that I had quit the fight because I had been wounded in battle. As a result, I had become a coward and had run away from the battle, but He put me back into the fight and made me an even stronger warrior than I had been before. Maybe that needs to happen to you. You may have been disappointed and discouraged, and you did not understand about the laws of restitution.

In the good confession of Jesus Christ we see that His faith was the deepest response of His heart to His Father. True faith is a demonstration of love worked out in the details of obedience.

Just pray:

Lord, I want to be like Jesus. Not only in the beauty of His gentleness and His other lovely attributes, but I want to be like Jesus in terms of His fighting faith. I want to fight the good fight of faith along with Him. I want to maintain the good confession like Jesus.

Thank you for the apostle Paul. He learned fighting faith from Jesus. Thank you for Timothy, for he learned it from Paul. I want to learn it from these great men as well. But most of all, I want to take Jesus as my glorious example and live like Him. I thank You that through Your eternal life You have given us the very faith that belongs to God so that we can fight a good fight of faith.

I want Your faith, not to receive bigger cars and more comfortable homes, but to see the Word of God manifested here in my city. I want to see my community broken open for the Kingdom of God. I want to see the devil defeated and destroyed on every side.

Deposit this faith into my spirit, in Jesus' mighty name.

Amen.

You may want to pray your own private prayer telling God what you are going to do in response to this truth. Tell Him how you are going to live differently. Let Him speak to you about your life and show you how He wants you to respond.

CHAPTER 7

GREAT FAITH

In the New Testament, we only read of two people that Jesus acknowledged as having great faith. One was a Roman centurion and the other a Canaanite woman. Both came to Jesus on behalf of somebody else. The Canaanite woman came to Jesus seeking deliverance for her demonized daughter (see Matt. 15:21-28). The Roman centurion sent for Jesus to heal his sick servant (see Luke 7:1-9).

It is interesting to note that neither of them were Jews. I am often asked to explain why God seems to do more miracles in Africa and India than in many western Christian nations. I have come to the conclusion that too many western Christians have become part of a church life that is all too familiar with a non-powerful Jesus, just like the people of His hometown of Nazareth.

> *Now He could do no mighty work there, except that He laid His hands on a few sick people and healed them. And He marveled because of their unbelief... (Mark 6:5-6).*

The problem with the people in Nazareth was that they had known Jesus from the time He was a little boy right through to manhood, and for those 30 years, He had done nothing powerful because His time had not yet come. They could not believe that Jesus, with whom they were so familiar, was now different, that He had returned with power to do mighty miracles and destroy all the works of the evil one.

One of the biggest problems we face is unbelief. In spite of years of faithful church attendance, the Jesus of power and miracles is a total stranger to many. Just like the people in Nazareth, many regular church members have only known a non-powerful Jesus and have never seen a miracle.

THE AUTHORITY OF FAITH

Great faith comes by obeying God's word. In Luke 7:1-8, we read of a Roman centurion who made Jesus marvel. He alone seemed to understand the principle by which Jesus lived. This was because of his military background. In his military training, the first thing he learned was to obey unconditionally every word that was spoken to him through his superior officers as if it came directly from Caesar himself.

In verse 8 the centurion said,

"For I also am a man placed under authority, having soldiers under me. And I say to one, 'Go,' and he goes; and to another, 'Come,' and he comes; and to my servant, 'Do this,' and he does it." When Jesus heard these things, He marveled at him, and turned around and said to the crowd that followed Him, "I say to you, I have not found such great faith, not even in Israel!" (Luke 7:8-9).

This quality of obedience is the key to great faith. If you want to get into great faith, then you better learn the key:

Faith does not begin by speaking God's Word. It begins by first learning the power of His Word though obeying His Word!

Many years ago, I was drafted into the British Royal Air Force. At that time, Great Britain was ruled by King George VI. It was February 13, 1949, when I stood on a freezing cold parade ground in my new Air Force uniform with a bunch of rookies just like me. There I had my first experience with a drill sergeant. I have not forgotten what he said, even to this day. He said, "Listen you lot! You are now in His Majesty's Air Force. If you get any sleep, it's a privilege. If you get any pay, it's a privilege. If you get any food, it's a privilege. You are His Majesty's property 24 hours a day, and he can do what he likes with you! Do you understand that?"

"Yes, Sergeant!" we all replied.

Then the sergeant came up to me, looked at me closely, and said, "Sonny! Did you shave this morning?" I said, "No, Sergeant, I only need to shave once every three days." He said, "Listen, His Majesty requires you to shave every morning whether you need it or not. Get shaved!" From that day on I had to go through the motions of shaving nothing every morning so as to please the king!

On our first day each one of us was given a big book, bigger than my Bible. On the front cover was the title, *King's Regulations*. Inside were thousands of regulations listing all the things the king commanded me to do and all the things the king forbade me to do. My whole life now was to be governed by His Majesty's Regulations. I had to cut my hair the way His Majesty wanted me to. I had to get up when he wanted me up. Every piece of clothing I wore and every part of my life was now regulated by the king.

In a few weeks, we had pretty well memorized these regulations, and they had now become part of us. As the word did its work in us, we literally became the word of the king made flesh. We would tell each other continuously, "You can't do that; it's not King's Regulations," or, "You must do this; it is King's Regulations." It was amazing how this group of undisciplined, rebellious, independent teenagers became a disciplined, dangerous fighting force in just a few weeks, as they learned the power of obedience to the word of the king.

If you were particularly smart and disciplined, then you could be promoted to officer training. In officer training, the regulations did not get easier. They got even more severe. The whole purpose of this training was to see if you would follow an appointed leader and obey his orders exactly in all circumstances. As an officer cadet, you never gave orders throughout the entire training period. You just learned to obey every word in all circumstances. You were deliberately put through some very provoking circumstances to see if there was any rebellion in you or whether you would make independent decisions and act contrary to orders. If an officer cadet failed these tests, then he was taken off the course as "unsuitable officer material." Obeying orders, even more than courage or initiative, was what qualified a person to become an officer in His Majesty's Air Force. If they could find implicit obedience in you, then you would eventually be trusted with the king's authority.

After passing every test, you became a commissioned officer in His Majesty's Air Force. Then, and only then, for the first time, some men were put under your authority, and they were expected to obey you in the same way. You were given this authority because you had first proved that you knew how to be under authority.

The centurion who came to Jesus was probably trained in a similar way and was able to see that this was also the key to Jesus' authority. When that centurion spoke to a soldier all the authority of Caesar was behind what he said. They obeyed him because the power of Rome was behind his every word. He would say, "Go!" and they went, "Come!" and they came (see Luke 7:8). This centurion knew perfectly well that when he spoke as Caesar's representative, all the power of Rome was behind the words he spoke. The centurion had first learned to implicitly obey every word without argument or question and to come completely under Caesar's authority. Now when he spoke Caesar's word, it never occurred to him that anyone would dare to disobey that word.

In the same way, we are trained in the power of God's Word by obedience. Only when we have learned to obey God's Word implicitly are we able to speak His Word with authority. You will never have authority to speak the Word until you yourself have learned its full power by obedience. This is the way God brings us to great faith.

The centurion understood this principle: "Lord, You don't need to come; just speak the word, and my servant will be healed. For I too (like You) am a man under authority, with soldiers under me" (see Luke 7:6-8). This man saw that Jesus also was a man under authority. However, Jesus was under the greater authority of Almighty God. Because of Jesus' perfect obedience, living every day only to do His Father's will, His Father had given Him authority over all things and all the power of Heaven was behind everything

Jesus said. The centurion grasped this principle of faith and authority while all the religious theologians were hotly debating the issue of Jesus' authority (see Matt. 21:23). This man perceived a spiritual principle in one moment. Jesus said of him, *This man has great faith,* and instantly his servant was healed (see Luke 7:9-10).

The centurion saw that Jesus lived a perfect life of obedience to God's authority. He said, "I see in You a man who lives under the authority of Almighty God. You live by every word that comes out of the mouth of God." The centurion reasoned correctly: "I know about authority in the military realm, but You evidently know all about a much greater authority in every realm."

Jesus had lived obediently for thirty years before the day finally came when He was anointed with the Holy Spirit and with power in the river Jordan. He was then commissioned by the Father to go out as a man with authority because He had proved for thirty years that He was a man under authority. For that reason, He had all the authority of Heaven behind everything that He did and every word that He spoke. (See Matthew 3:1-17.)

FAITH IS PRACTICAL AND MUST BE PERSISTENT

In John chapter 7 Jesus said,

*If anyone **wills** to do His will, he shall know concerning the doctrine, whether it is from God or whether I speak on My own authority* (John 7:17).

The only way to prove that God's Word really is God's Word is to doggedly do it! This requires much more than just a short-term, half-hearted effort. It will require your entire will and being to persist until it comes to pass. When going through military training, you have to apply all your will in order to complete a 25-mile march through the mud. God will put you through similar situations spiritually to train you. At times the Holy Spirit is just like a drill sergeant. He wants to bring some of us to officer level in faith so that we can speak God's Word with power and authority. We will not reach that place without going through a rigorous training program. We have to will to do His will.

For example, to test your faithfulness with tithes and offerings, God will put you through a practical test. It is easy to tithe when you have plenty of money, but what happens when you don't. Does God's Word change? Of course not! What if you are in financial trouble? Spiritually it might seem like slogging knee-deep through mud to give your tithes and offerings, but you must keep going, and eventually God will gloriously answer.

Six weeks after my wife and I were saved, we saw in Scripture the need to give tithes and offerings. We were not going to a church that taught it, but it was so clear in the Bible that we decided to do it. So, very early in our Christian lives we began to learn the faithfulness of God.

When we went to India, we had no mission society sending us and had no human means of financial support. We had no choice but to trust God completely. We went, just trusting God, because God told us to go. That was not easy to do, but God proved Himself to be utterly faithful. The "School of Faith" is not easy, but the fruit is enormous.

We came home to Britain after all those years in India. I was well qualified in my field of expertise, and there were plenty of jobs at that time. I could easily have found a well-paying job, but I was under authority. God said, *"No, I want you to be in the ministry. I want you to build this little church."*

The only problem was that this little church could not pay me. In fact, they had no understanding of giving, and, therefore, we had little or no money. I would go to meetings, and I would preach my heart out. At the end they would say, "Thank you very much, that was wonderful," and that was it! They would give me nothing. They would drive off in nice cars to lovely Sunday lunches, and I would drive home in a rusty old van to very little to eat at times. I found myself getting very resentful toward these people that I was trying to pastor, and God had to really deal with my heart.

One day God said to me, *"Are you preaching for money or are you preaching out of obedience?"* I said, "Well, I know what the Bible says, and I want to have the right attitude, but I'm finding it very hard in these circumstances." I went through a hard and rigorous training to come to faith about these things. Sometimes we had nothing to eat. Once, in her desperation, Eileen decided to fast for ten days, which was not so hard since there wasn't much to eat anyway. She cried out to God, "Lord, please send some supply!"

At that same time, we discovered that our house had an infestation of woodworm, a wood-eating beetle that is a little bit like a termite. We needed to get it treated, and it was going to cost a lot of money, but I had nothing. I prayed, "Lord, I need to get this treated. Please send the money." The Lord said, *"Get them to do it and I'll pay."* I answered, "I have never written a check without the money in the bank. I cannot do that. It's not honorable." The Lord replied, *"Do it this once, and I will not fail you."*

I went through this battle for three weeks, and all the time we had almost nothing to eat. Finally, Eileen asked, "Why don't you go and get some work?" I told her, "I would love to, but God is not permitting me to do that." I was now neck deep in the mud, slogging through this terrible situation, thinking to myself, *"Let's get out of this faith business. Let me just go back to work and earn a good, comfortable living."*

This whole trial had been going on for about seven months. At one point, all we had to eat for three weeks was a sack of potatoes that some Christian farmer friend had dropped at our front door. We simply ate those potatoes and nothing else all that time. I came to the point where I thought I could not even preach anymore, and I was reaching the breaking point. I was shut in by God.

God was telling me to get that woodworm fixed in our house, but I still refused to do it without having the money in my hands first. I knew I had to call the men to begin the treatment, but I knew I would have to write a check when they finished the work. I felt God assuring me that He would not let the check bounce, but it was totally against all my principles to do such a thing. (And I'm certainly not recommending you take such an action unless God specifically speaks to you.)

This was so against my lifestyle that I continued to say, "No Lord, I can't do it. Send the money first and then I'll write the check." But God said, *"No, I want to teach you something about faith. You write the check, and I'll send the money. You trust Me to get the money in before the check bounces."*

I answered faintly, "Lord this hurts!" He said, *"Exactly, but I'm going to turn you into a man of faith even if it almost kills you."* This reminded me of my drill sergeant. I was being disciplined by a stern Jesus who I did not know very well. I knew the loving, gentle Jesus, but when God wants to get you to some new place of faith, He can arrange some tough situations, and yet it's still His perfect love at work.

I finally called the company. They immediately sent their workers who went all over the house treating the woodworm. When they finished, they handed me the bill, and I took a deep breath as I wrote the check. We did not even have money to buy a gallon of gas for our little rusty old van. The tank was completely empty, and I was walking everywhere.

At that particular time in England, we were getting a small "child allowance" from the government for each one of our three children. We received this allowance weekly, and in those days it amounted to about $20.00 for all three. In our most severe trials, we always faithfully tithed this little bit of money. I used some of this money to buy a little gas for the van because I had been invited to preach at another church on Sunday. However, I could only buy enough gas to get us to the church. We did not have enough to get back home again. Even if the church gave me a check immediately, it would not put gas in our vehicle on Sunday.

I said to my wife, "At least we'll get a decent lunch." Since it was Sunday, I knew they would do something special. While we were driving there, I said to our children,

"We're going to have a fantastic lunch today. Eat all you can because we're not sure where the next meal is coming from."

As we drove to the meeting Eileen said, "Something is really bothering me." I said, "What's that?" She said, "Here we are going to church, and I have nothing to give to the Lord to show Him how much I love Him and thank Him for all He has done for me. I'm going to ask God to somehow send me some money even now, so I can give Him a thank offering." I shrugged my shoulders and thought, *I've got much bigger things to worry about.*

When we got to the church, a man walked up to Eileen in the parking lot and gave her a cash gift equivalent to about $200 today. She was ecstatic and said, "Look what the Lord has done! He has given me an offering." I said, "What are you going to do with it?" She replied, "This is my offering. I'm going to give it all to the Lord." I cried out in protest, "You can't do that! We need the money." She said, "No, this is what I asked for. It's my offering. Let me give it to the Lord."

We went into the service, and when it came to offering time, I watched as Eileen put it all in the offering. I'll never forget the look of absolute joy on her face as she did it. As I watched I was deeply convicted that, although I was a faithful regular giver, I knew nothing about a heart that would rather give than eat. I asked God to change my heart to make it as generous as hers.

Eileen was behaving just like the widow woman who gave the two mites, all she had, into the offering in the temple. Jesus said she went down more justified than the rich Pharisee who gave in a showy way out of his abundance (see

Mark 12:42–44). It was this act of abandoned giving that broke the financial drought over our lives.

We had two great meetings with a wonderful lunch beyond our wildest expectations. After the evening meeting, the church gave me a check. It was a generous gift, but not enough to pay for the woodworm treatment. Nor did we have any cash to buy gas on the way home. Then one of the elders said to me, "I would like you to come home to my house before you leave. I'd like to have some fellowship with you." He drove off in his brand-new Mercedes, and I followed him in my rusty old van.

We went to his house and talked while his wife was in the kitchen preparing some refreshments. Then we received the shock of our lives. This has never happened before or since, just on this one occasion. While his wife was in the kitchen and we were talking in the living room, unbeknownst to us, the lady of the house went into their storage room and pulled out a large cardboard box and took it into the kitchen. She then unloaded everything from their larder, refrigerator, and freezer, including fresh milk, and filled this large box to overflowing. Then she staggered in with it and said, "I hope you won't be offended, but I just felt the Lord tell me to do this. So I've emptied out my larder, refrigerator, and freezer into this box. Then He told me to empty out my purse, put all the money into this box, and give it to you."

Amazingly, there was even toothpaste in the box. I had not seen toothpaste for weeks. There were many items we had been unable to buy, including toilet paper. I won't tell you how we managed, but as missionaries we knew how to cope in these circumstances.

Finally, at the end of our fellowship time this man pulled out his checkbook and wrote a large check that was exactly the amount I needed to pay for the woodworm treatment! The test was over, and we had passed. So then God lavished upon us everything we needed. We had cash to buy gas on the way home, ample fresh food for our immediate needs, and a check that would pay every bill and give us an adequate supply of money for the future.

That was a long time ago, and we have never been put through a test like that again. These kinds of tests do not need to happen more than once, provided we learn the lessons. It's just like doing a college course. If you do the course and pass the test at the end of the course, then you don't have to repeat the course. But if you fail, you have to do it again. The "School of Faith" is like that, and God will take you through the course again if you don't pass the test. It's much better to pass the first time.

The Holy Spirit is more rigorous and more thorough than any drill sergeant. He longs to bring you to great faith. My question to you is, how much do you really want to become a man or a woman of great faith? If you will complete the training, then you will be able to speak God's Word with all His authority and get some great answers to your prayers.

I am still learning and growing in faith. As I mentioned, I once had an evil heart of unbelief when it came to healing, but it's gone. I long to be like that centurion so I can make Jesus marvel in every respect. That is my ambition. I am not so concerned about people. I want to be pleasing to Him. Wouldn't it be wonderful if Jesus could say of some of us, "I haven't seen such great faith, not in all America!" Isn't it worth going through those rigorous training exercises that may make you sweat and hurt and strain every spiritual muscle if they bring you to great faith? Isn't the pain of the trial worth the fruit of great faith that will afterward flow out of our lives?

GREAT FAITH OF DESPERATE LOVE

Matthew 15:21-28 describes the other person who Jesus greatly commended for her faith. However, before we look at this, I want us to look at the story of another woman in order to compare the completely different way in which Jesus treated the two women and understand why He did so.

WIDOW OF NAIN

Immediately following the story of the centurion, Luke tells us the story of the widow of Nain. In Luke 7:11-16, Jesus comes across a funeral procession which is taking the body of the only son of a widow woman to be buried. She is wailing with grief, and so is everyone in the crowd. She is facing an unbearable situation. First her husband and now her son have died, leaving her with no one to comfort her or to provide for her.

Jesus was so touched by this tragic situation that He was moved with compassion and decided to do something about it. There was no faith in the woman and no faith in the crowd of mourners. So Jesus decided to use His own faith to do a mighty miracle to meet this woman's desperate need. He stopped the funeral procession, touched the coffin, and commanded the young man to arise. The young man was immediately raised from the dead. The crowd went crazy, and the widow woman went home with her resurrected son with great joy and thanksgiving. (See Luke 7:11-16.)

This widow woman contributed nothing to the miracle and was simply the grateful beneficiary of the faith, power, and tender compassion of Jesus. She did not use any faith of her own; neither did the crowd contribute anything to this amazing miracle. It was the compassion, faith, and power of Jesus alone. Because the widow did not exercise faith in this instance, her own faith did not develop through this crisis, though Jesus' compassion and power may have ignited faith in her for the future. The amazing, tender compassion that Jesus had for this helpless, needy woman reveals to us the true heart of our wonderful Savior.

CANAANITE WOMAN

Now let's move on to the other story recorded in Matthew 15:21-28.

Then Jesus went out from there and departed to the region of Tyre and Sidon. And behold, a woman of Canaan came from that region and cried out to Him, saying, "Have mercy on me, O Lord, Son of David! My daughter is severely demon-possessed" (Matthew 15:21-22).

The disciples had no time for her and said, "Send her away, for she's making such a dreadful noise" (see Matt. 15:23). Jesus did not even bother to answer her. In the face of such a response, most people would have been very discouraged.

Jesus had not behaved like that to the centurion or to the widow of Nain. When the centurion sent for Him, He immediately went with them. When the widow of Nain was crying out in deep distress, Jesus acted without her even having to ask Him. But He seemed to treat this Canaanite woman in an entirely different way, even with seeming indifferent harshness. It is important that we see why.

In verse 23 it says that Jesus "answered her not a word" (Matt. 15:23). We must recognize that His seeming indifference was deliberate. There was a reason for it. He saw something in her that He had not seen in the widow of Nain. As He deliberately ignored this woman, He said to Himself, *This woman has great tenacity and a great faith potential. If I make it tough for her, she's not going to give up. I'm going to develop her into a mighty warrior of faith just by making things tough for her.* Look at the process, the series of trials He took her through in order to draw out her great faith.

Obstacle #1: The Silence Test

Jesus answered her not a word. He completely ignored her. God will take us through times of distress where He doesn't seem to care or respond to our cries for help. That's the first test you have to go through. You have to praise Him and believe in Him when nothing works and it seems like He doesn't care.

A pastor was jailed for years in the worst days of communism in Romania. While in prison, he wrote sermons to himself that were later published as a book entitled, *A Series of Sermons in Prison.* While he was there, his wife and children were kicked out of their home; no one from the church was allowed to take them in; no one was allowed to feed them; and they were left out wandering around the streets like hungry dogs. When he read the Scriptures, it seemed like God didn't care, and he told God, "You seem to be violating every promise You have ever made in Scripture. But, I can't stop believing in You."

Sometimes this happens. You get to that position where nothing is working, nothing is happening, God doesn't seem to respond or answer, and you think this whole Christianity thing is a farce. Nevertheless, there is something inside you that will not stop believing. That is part of the process. God is growing something in you that will become a very powerful weapon of faith.

Jesus answered the Canaanite woman not a word. The woman's response was to get more desperate. She didn't care what it looked like. She didn't care what it sounded like. She was going to get an answer. She was like a British bulldog. When bulldogs sink their teeth into something, they never let go. Her response was to cry all the more loudly, not caring what anybody thought. God is bringing men and women into travail in order to bring things to birth in the spirit. While they are in this travail, they are not going to be careful about the way they behave. You may have to decide whether you want them in your meeting or not. When a woman is giving birth to a baby, she is not worried about what her hair looks like or what sort of noise she is making. She has other things occupying her attention. She's giving birth. She is totally focused on the responsibility to bring something new and glorious into this world. When you are gripped by travailing prayer, whether you are a man or woman, there is something of the same experience going on. It's noisy, it's messy, and it's often uncomfortable for the observers.

You may not understand what's going on, but you had better not interfere. If you let that travail go on, it may birth something that will transform your city. Men, as well as women, are being gripped by the spirit of travail. When men start to travail in prayer, revival is near. It's beginning to happen in America. For a long time, as a man you felt strange in prayer conferences because there was hardly another man there, but things are changing. Thank God for that. That is a sign of revival.

Obstacle #2: Reproach and Hostility

And His disciples came and urged Him, saying, "Send her away, for she cries out after us" (Matthew 15:23).

Not only was Jesus ignoring her, but His disciples were annoyed by her noisy persistence and asked Him to send her away. However, she didn't even acknowledge the reproach and hostility she encountered. The burden she was carrying mattered more to her than the opinions of those around her. She pursued Jesus with a singularity of purpose. No one was going to dissuade or distract her, and nothing was going to stop her from getting an answer.

Obstacle #3: Theological Roadblock

The account continues in verse 24 where Jesus responded,

"I was not sent except to the lost sheep of the house of Israel" (Matthew 15:24).

The third obstacle that Jesus deliberately put in her path was a theological one. Did she, a Gentile, have any right to ask Jesus, a Jew, to heal her daughter? Notice her wise response; she doesn't come back with a theological counter-argument, but with a desperate pleading heart. Today many different theological roadblocks are being raised to prevent people from freely asking and believing that Jesus will heal them. Others are being dissuaded from spiritual warfare by false theological positions. I will not try to enumerate them in this book. If you are desperate like this woman, you won't try to argue theology; you will just plead your way past every obstacle.

When they tried to get rid of her, she moved closer to Jesus.

Then she came and worshiped Him, saying, "Lord, help me!" (Matthew 15:25).

There are some additional precious insights in the Greek text that I want to bring out here. The Greek word used for worship in verse 25 is *proskuneo*, which literally means "to be dog-like toward." If you've ever had a dog that was really part of the family, then you will be able to understand what is being said here. When such a dog really wants something from its master, it will come to him with a whimper and pleading eyes. It will touch him gently with its paw until it gets what it wants. Such "worship" is almost impossible to resist. We had a black Labrador dog called Penny who would behave in this way whenever she smelled ice cream. I would tell the children not to give her any. Recognizing that I was the source of her problem, she would come directly to me and "worship" me until I gave in and let her have some ice cream. Our children would laugh at me because I couldn't resist such pleading worship. I always gave in. This is evidently what this woman did to Jesus. She worshipped Him like a dog and said, "Please, Lord, help me." This may well explain the next answer Jesus gave.

Obstacle #4: The Offense Test

> But He answered and said, "It is not good to take the children's bread and throw it to the little dogs" (Matthew 15:26).

This was the final test. In response to her dog-like worship, Jesus called her a dog! At this point most people would have walked off highly offended. *"This Jesus, a Jew, just called me a Gentile dog!"* But this woman refused to be put off and would not let go. She meekly responded,

> *"Yes, Lord, yet even the little dogs eat the crumbs which fall from their masters' table"* (Matthew 15:27).

I can then imagine Jesus bursting into laughter and saying, "Woman, great is your faith! You've passed every test. Go your way; your daughter is healed."

Jesus finally responded to this woman's perseverance and her refusal to take offence. He knew what was in this woman's heart, and He was treating her this way because He wanted to bring out the jewel of "great faith" that was hidden inside. Jesus was not really hard or indifferent, neither was He hostile because she was a Gentile and He was a Jew, although it seemed like it. In fact, He was paying her a great compliment by making it deliberately hard for her. He said these things because He saw a tenacious "bulldog faith" in this woman's heart that He wanted to bring out and mature. His purpose was to bring her faith to maturity, so she could use it again and again in the future.

If Jesus had immediately said, "I'll come and heal your daughter," we would never have found out what was in this woman's heart. Just after this incident, we read that a whole multitude came to Him and He healed them all (see Matt. 15:29-30). Jesus was not short of compassion or healing power. He would not heal this woman's daughter the easy way because He wanted to give her the full opportunity to use her "great faith." She could now go away and use that same faith to win many other battles on behalf of many other needy people.

This may explain why some of you reading this book are having a tough time trying to get yourself or someone else whom you love healed. You need to cry out with the same tenacity of faith that was in the heart of this woman so you can stick in there until you get the answer.

Once you've obtained your answer and learned the ways of "great faith," you can use that same faith to get many others healed and whole cities transformed.

DESPERATION FOR YOUR CITY

I first landed in Mumbai, India, in February 1963. We moved to a relatively poor area of town. Within a short time I had been lied to, spat on, cheated, and robbed. After a few weeks, I was offended and said to myself, "These people deserve to go to hell!" In a few weeks my heart of compassion for the nation of India had evaporated.

In this way, my true nature was being exposed, and I was discovering the hardness in my own heart. I knew it was wrong, and so I asked God to deal with it. There were only two options: The Lord had to get me out of that place, or He had to radically change me because I couldn't stay there as I was. I cried out to God, and He changed me.

He impacted my heart with something of what He felt for the city of Mumbai. I broke down and cried profusely. I sobbed with a broken heart. This same spirit came upon a group of not more than twelve or fifteen of us. We were broken up for Mumbai, crying out to God for its desperate need. God first laid hold of us for the city, and then we were able to lay hold of Him for the city.

The pursuit of God for our city led many of us to be baptized in the Holy Spirit. It was pure desperation! If you are desperate, then you stop bothering about theological issues. You simply want God to do something. When you are desperate, you do not argue about what is the correct way to pray in the Spirit; you just pray!

God visited us in Mumbai. Some of those who were saved in those days now have powerful ministries. They have planted hundreds of churches in Mumbai and across India. That small praying group in India had the same heart as the Canaanite woman. The badly demonized city was like their daughter. God can bring you to a point where you love a lost city like your own daughter. All the ills that curse a city have their origin in demonic activity. God will visit a city if a few little "nobodies" will cry out to Him with a heart like the Canaanite woman. God can grab hold of them and make them His instrument to bring transformation to any city.

Recently, as God began to speak to me about other cities, I had to confess to Him, "Lord, I've lost that heart, but I want it back again. I don't cry the way I used to. I've become professional and knowledgeable. I want that woman's heart again. That kind of heart is more precious than any knowledge or skill you can acquire, and that kind of heart will bring transformation to your city.

LETTING GO OF RESPECTABILITY

When Jesus did not answer one word, this woman refused to be quiet but cried out all the more. You never know when the travail is going to come. You come to a place where you don't care what you look like or what it sounds like. I was raised as a respectable Englishman, and I did not like to be emotional or to be seen crying in public. I had to deal with this before God. Now I would rather see God shake my city than keep my respectability.

The disciples disapproved of her outburst and said, "Get rid of this woman who is always crying out" (see Matt. 15:23). The person who is carrying a burden can present problems in a meeting for some. They may start crying and praying loudly at the wrong time, and people will say, "Oh, get rid of her. She is disturbing the meeting." We need to be careful not to react the same way. If this is a genuine burden from God and we quench it, then we may prevent the birth of the very thing we are longing for, which is a transformed city.

I'm praying and waiting for Jesus to transform the city of San Antonio, which is where I live. I want to feel for this city what I felt for Mumbai. I cry out to God, "I want that woman's heart." He wants us to have that heart, but it is not possible for us to manufacture it. We can only open our hearts and let Him give us His desires and burdens.

CRY OUT TO GOD

Oh God, our city is severely demonized. Every institution is controlled by the demonic. Such wickedness! Our younger generation is being destroyed. Families are torn apart. There is such violence. Terrible things go on in the schools. Our politics are so polluted with demonic darkness. Oh God! Heal this city! Spread out across this country and across this nation."

Call out to God for this heart of great faith. Cry out to God for the discipline of the soldier and the compassion of this woman.

God, we ask You to put these two attitudes of heart together and make us men and women of great faith. Lord, it comes from You, and we want Your love to grip us. We want to feel what You feel for our city. Lord, change us so that we will truly be "city takers" and "nation changers!"

⊰ CHAPTER 8 ⊱

BEAN SPROUT TO FRUIT TREE FAITH

GAINING A POSITION OF
PERMANENT FRUITFULNESS IN FAITH

At the end of John chapter 4 and the beginning of John chapter 5, two miracles are recorded consecutively. They are two great miracles individually, but they are put together because they teach us one important principle. We must learn how to move from a faith that depends on others to help us, to a place where we have learned to stand on our own feet and obtain what we need entirely on our own in all circumstances.

In the beginning of John 4, Jesus goes out of His way to meet a Samaritan woman who is a social outcast in her own village because of her immoral behavior. She has a mighty encounter with Jesus that saves her and transforms her. She then runs into her village and tells them all the wonderful things He has done for her and brings them all to meet her Savior (see John 4:7-39). After listening to Jesus, they make this important statement:

Now we believe, not because of what you said, for we ourselves have heard Him and we know that this is indeed the Christ, the Savior of the world (John 4:42).

It is very important that we learn this lesson and do not leave people in a state of only believing because of what we have told them. This is especially true of our own natural children and others that we may have led to Christ. They are not secure until they have come to the place where they have seen Jesus and heard Him for themselves. Then their faith will be able to stand against all the devil's attacks of doubt.

LEANING FAITH

Immediately afterward, John tells the story of the first of these two miracles. A certain nobleman whose son was sick came and implored Jesus to heal his son who was at the point of death. Jesus responds by saying, "Unless you people see signs and wonders, you will by no means believe" (John 4:48).

What Jesus is saying to this man and to people like him is that this "faith" of his is not real faith at all because it depends upon being in an atmosphere where the natural senses are being encouraged to believe by seeing what is already happening to others. This is what I have come to call "leaning faith" because it depends heavily on the presence of the right environment. Once that environment is removed, the "faith" often turns to doubt, and the healing which was temporarily experienced is frequently lost. I have seen this happen a lot in big healing crusade meetings.

Jesus wanted to bring this man to real faith so instead of going with him, He just said, "Go your way, your son lives" (John 4:50). This put the man right on the spot. He had a choice to make. Was he going to believe the word spoken to him, or was he going to go on pleading with Jesus to come? He made the decision to believe, and this required him to walk away from the physical presence of Jesus and begin simply walking on the word he had received.

THE SEED IS THE WORD

All true faith is produced by the Word of God. There is no other source. Jesus explained this very carefully in the parable of the sower, with which He began all His other teaching parables in all three synoptic Gospels. He plainly states that "if you don't understand this parable, you will not understand any of the others." (See Matthew 13; Mark 4; and Luke 8.) The seed is variously described as the Word of God, the Word of the Kingdom, or just the Word. It is planted in four kinds of soil, and each kind of soil represents a different heart condition. The seed germinates in three cases and comes to different degrees of harvest in two cases.

Five things characterize the heart that will see the Word fulfilled in a hundredfold harvest. If the first three are present, a measure of harvest will be experienced, but not the full hundredfold. A heart that will experience a measure of the harvest is a heart which

1. Hears the Word.

2. Understands the Word.

3. Accepts the Word.

In order to reap the full hundredfold harvest two additional things are necessary. These are described only in Luke's version. In addition, one must

4. Hold the Word fast.

5. Persevere in it.

In other words, it requires long-term perseverance to reap the full hundredfold harvest.

As the nobleman began his long walk home, the seed of the Word germinated in his heart. At first he didn't feel any different and was still gripped by the same fears and anxiety. But gradually, as the journey continued and as he persevered, the seed grew within his spirit, and it came to harvest. By the time he came close to home, he was already dancing with joy, and when his servants met him he wasn't a bit surprised with the news: "Your son lives" (John 4:51). He simply enquired at what time it happened and found it was the same hour that he believed (see John 4:52-53).

BEAN SPROUT FAITH

Many of us will remember as little children an early biology lesson in which we took some bean sprout seeds and pushed them into blotting paper, which had been wet with a solution of nutrients, and then placed them in jars containing a solution of nutrients. We watched with wonder as the seeds sprouted long roots within 24 hours. By the end of about three days, these bean sprouts had come to harvest and were ready to eat. Teachers often use bean sprout seeds to demonstrate these principles because the attention span of a young child is very short.

When I was a very small boy, my father gave me a small piece of the garden to try growing some vegetables. He showed me how to prepare the ground one Saturday morning. We sowed some carrot and lettuce seeds, and I carefully covered them over and watered them. I watched the plot all day, and I went to bed very disappointed when nothing had happened. The next morning I got up early and ran quickly to my garden. Still nothing had happened, so frustrated, I churned the ground over with my shoes in my deep disappointment.

Many Christians behave in a similar way spiritually when it comes to faith. They pray "in faith," but if something does not happen quickly, their "faith" fades away. They pray on Sunday and expect a result immediately or by Wednesday at the latest. If it doesn't happen that quickly, they give up in disappointment. These Christians only have what I call "bean sprout faith."

"Bean sprout faith" is not a bad thing because it does see some results in a limited way, but it is the faith of the immature, and it will not be able to obtain the many things that do not come to harvest so quickly.

GRAIN HARVEST FAITH

Farmers who grow various grain crops are not so fool-ish. They know it takes time to get a harvest. They are pre-pared to work to prepare the ground, then sow, then work, and then wait for about another four months to get a har-vest. Moreover, once the harvest is reaped, they know they will have to repeat the whole process all over again the next spring to get another harvest.

What I have come to call "grain harvest faith" is the most common kind of faith to be found in most churches. When there is a crisis such as a life-threatening illness or another dangerous situation threatening one of the mem-bers, a group in the church will gather together for special prayer and will persevere for several months, sometimes until the crisis is over. Once their prayers have been heard over this particular matter, the group disbands until another crisis comes.

This "grain harvest faith" is a lot better than "bean sprout faith," and it will see many successes, but Jesus wants us to copy Him and go even further. Jesus wants us to grow in faith until we have what I like to call "fruit tree faith."

FRUIT TREE FAITH

On another occasion when I was a small boy, I was eating an apple, and I asked my dad about the seeds in the apple. He explained that these were potentially new apple trees. If we planted them in the ground, they would germinate, and they would eventually grow into apple trees. So I decided to try this and planted a lot of these seeds in my garden.

Sure enough, some months later a few of them did germinate and some little tiny green shoots appeared. Some died, but some went on growing and eventually after several years became tiny apple trees, but there was no fruit. So I asked my dad, and he said, "Just wait and see. Eventually some of them may become fruitful."

Altogether it took about ten to twelve years, but finally a few of them began to produce apples just like the seed that had been sown. Once they began to bear fruit, they continued to be fruitful every year for the rest of their lives. When the last family member left that house about 50 years later, they had become large, magnificent fruit trees bearing an enormous amount of fruit every year.

It may take time and many trials to get to this "fruit tree faith" level, but once we get there we can go on being fruitful in this area for the rest of our lives. Jesus was the perfect example of a great fruit-bearing faith tree. He was always ready to meet every need at any time. He didn't have to go away and pray and prepare Himself. He was always ready because He lived a life of prayer and fasting.

TOUGH LOVE OF JESUS

As we have already seen with the Canaanite woman, Jesus can be really tough with us in order to bring us to great faith. John continues straight on into chapter 5:1-9 with the story of the second of these two miracles. Jesus goes to a pool in Jerusalem where a great multitude of sick and lame people are gathered waiting for a supernatural moving of the waters (see John 5:1-4).

This scenario is a tragic picture of the Church in many places in America and other western countries. The pool was situated at the Sheep Gate and was where the sheep gathered. It had a covering supported by five pillars, which symbolize the five-fold ministries. The pool was called Bethesda, which means "the house of kindness or the house of mercy." However, instead of being a flowing river that brought life wherever it went, it had become a stagnant pool. The multitude gathered around the pool represents the many needy people who have been going to church regularly, some of them for many years, hoping that one day they might have a special visitation from God and have their needs met. But it's only a vague hope with no faith and very little expectation in it.

The crowd was like today's typical loving church community that shows a lot of kindness and sympathy to many immature baby Christians but does not have any radical answers for this chronically needy group. In many churches, the pastoral care ministry is exactly like this. It pours out a lot of sympathy but does not have any real answers. After years of attending such churches, nothing has changed in this group, and no one is any different. They content themselves with praying for revival and hope that one day the Spirit may come and change everything. Until then, they can do nothing but wait.

Jesus walked into this scenario and went up to one man; in John 5:6, Jesus asked this man a direct question, "Do you want to be made well?" (John 5:6.)

The man's response was to make three excuses as to why it was not possible.

1. "I have no man to put me into the pool..." (John 5:7). He placed the responsibility on someone else's coming and being the right man on his behalf while he remained the passive beneficiary.

2. "When the water is stirred..." (John 5:7). This man could only conceive of special brief moments of opportunity. He thought, *You just have to be lucky enough to be in the right place at the right time.*

3. "Another steps down before me" (John 5:7). He saw a very limited grace opportunity. He had heard about others being blessed but didn't really expect it ever to be his turn.

Jesus responded with three short, sharp commandments. They are much stronger in the original Greek than they appear in our English Bibles. The first two commandments are in the present imperative tense, which means they are like a military order, and the point of time is right now!

Jesus didn't show any sympathy, He just barked these three orders at him.

1. *"Get up now!"* (see John 5:8). The man was so shocked to be spoken to in this way that he immediately leapt to his feet. He was standing on his own feet for the first time in 38 years.

As he stood there, the unreality and impossibility of what he was doing began to dawn on him. He began to look longingly at his bed, on which he had lain for the past 38 years, and wanted to go back there.

His bed represents the bed of excuses many Christians lie on to explain why they cannot live the victorious Christian life: *"I was so abused as a child. I've been through a disastrous divorce. I was so wounded in that terrible church split. I've always been told I was no good. My former drug life has disqualified me. I'm just glad Jesus has saved me but please don't expect me to be anything or do anything."*

2. Jesus then barked, *"Roll up your bed now!* (see John 5:8). You're never going to need that again. Don't you ever dare to try to lie down on it again.

3. His final commandment is still in the imperative, but it is also in the present continuous tense, which translates, *"Walk* and go on continually walking!" (see John 5:8). In other words, "Don't ever stop! Keep going!" In my imagination, I can see Jesus getting a stick and prodding the man, physically chasing him several times around the pool.

The man finally realizes he is totally cured and cries out, "I'm healed, I can walk." Jesus says, "Don't you ever go back and sin any more" (see John 5:14). This man's condition was a direct result of his former sinful life, but once he repented, he was free forever, provided he never went back to that sin.

Sometimes the most loving thing we can do for someone who is locked into a life of self-destructive, sinful habits (such as constant overeating) is to lovingly get tough with them like Jesus did and command them to "Get up! Roll up your bed and walk." Then the word can do its work, and we will have a church full of walking miracles, instead of needy, immature invalids. Then corporately we can stop our churches from just being stagnant pools, and we can become a river of life flowing into our city in order to transform it.

CHAPTER 9

MUSTARD SEED FAITH

In order to fight the good fight of faith, we must have a certain kind of faith. Jesus wants His disciples to have "Mustard Seed Faith." There are two key verses on this kind of faith. First, look at Matthew 17:

> *Then the disciples came to Jesus privately and said, "Why could we not cast it out?" So Jesus said to them, "Because of your unbelief; for assuredly, I say to you, if you have faith as a mustard seed, you will say to this mountain, 'Move from here to there,' and it will move; and nothing will be impossible for you. However, this kind does not go out except by prayer and fasting"* (Matthew 17:19-21).

Jesus did not say this casually. "Assuredly I say to you..." is a word of emphasis (Matt. 17:20). Jesus is stressing the importance of what He is about to say. The King James says, "verily I say unto you..." (Matt. 17:20 KJV). Jesus is saying, *Listen guys, I really mean what I am saying here. I cannot emphasize strongly enough how true this is.* He is emphasizing the importance of having mustard seed faith.

Now look at Matthew 13:

Another parable He put forth to them, saying: "The kingdom of heaven is like a mustard seed, which a man took and sowed in his field, which indeed is the least of all the seeds; but when it is grown it is greater than the herbs and becomes a tree, so that the birds of the air come and nest in its branches" (Matthew 13: 31-32).

"But when it is grown..." Whenever God does anything, He usually starts small, but it is in the nature of God that it does not remain small. It always gets bigger. When Jesus came into the world, He came in unobtrusively. No one knew about it except a few shepherds who were told by the angels. It would not have been given a single line in any newspaper, but in that little baby born in a manger was the power to destroy the whole of satan's kingdom. His coming was small and almost invisible, but it began a process that would change the whole world.

When the disciples gathered together in the upper room, it was just one room with one hundred and twenty people in it. It was not a big event, but the Spirit fell upon them, and in a matter of months they were shaking the city and then the whole world. They had no media, no modern methods of proclaiming the Gospel, but there was power in what they did.

In Mathew 13:31, Jesus compares the Kingdom of Heaven to a mustard seed and then describes it as the least of all the seeds. We are told a man took it and sowed it in his field. The field represents the world. The purpose of God is not to grow churches that quietly meet in buildings where nobody knows they exist, but to grow churches that burst forth visibly to impact society until the whole world knows about them. They may start small and be unobtrusive, but it is not God's plan for them to stay that way.

The mustard seed of God has some strange properties. Most notably, it has the ability to grow into a great tree. I have done some research on the various species of mustard and all varieties grow on bushes. I cannot find a single species of mustard seed that actually grows into a tree. A mustard seed that grows into a tree must be a special Kingdom variety that defies nature and obeys the higher law of God. For a great mustard tree to come out of the tiniest of seeds, which shouldn't grow into a tree at all, it has to have some unique supernatural properties.

The reason this tiny seed grows into a great tree is in the nature of the seed. When I go to a church, I don't care whether it is small or big. What I am looking for are the qualities that make it the kind of seed that will grow into a great tree no matter what natural limitations exist.

The parable in Matthew 13 is talking about the kind of church that will break free of natural limitations, penetrate the heavens, spread out its branches in the heavenlies, destroy principalities and powers, and change the very climate of the atmosphere over the city. When this seed is grown, instead of having the atmosphere of the kingdom of darkness over a city, we have the atmosphere of the Kingdom of Heaven coming down to Earth to replace it.

In the tea gardens of India, the rows of tea bushes have trees planted periodically between them. The trees grow up, spread out their branches, and provide a covering that protects the tea bushes from the burning heat of the sun during the day. Just imagine if all over the world in every city there were churches that were growing into great powerful churches, spreading their branches out in the heavens, touching one another, and locking their branches together until every nation was covered with a heavenly shade. Hallelujah!

There is another kind of church: one that grows into a bush. Most churches become bushes and never get any bigger. As they grow, they abide within their natural and spiritual limitations. These smaller churches would sit under the shade of the great city churches, and even they would prosper.

The mustard seed of God has the power to defy nature, grow into a great tree, fill the heavenlies with its branches, and bring a heavenly shade so that everything on Earth lives under its shade and protection. What is it that destines the mustard seed to become a great tree instead of an insignificant bush?

THE SEED MUST BE OF THE KINGDOM

There are two essential elements, and the rest flow out from it. First, the mustard seed must be of the Kingdom. Second, the mustard seed must be able to move mountains. Let's begin by looking at the Kingdom aspect of the mustard seed. The Kingdom of Heaven is like a mustard seed that can grow into a great tree. If you and your church were to fulfill the promises of God, it would be such big news that you wouldn't be able to keep the reporters away. God said that His Church is to become a city set on a hill that cannot be hidden. You could not hide it, even if you tried because of the power and glory that would flow out from it.

The mustard seed is of the Kingdom. To fully explain the Kingdom would take a very large separate book, but all I want to do here is expose the heart and essence of the Kingdom. It is very, very simple. What does it mean for the Kingdom of God to come? It means that the rule of God comes. The word *Kingdom* means "rule." The rule, or the government of God has come.

The Kingdom is essentially a relationship where God rules and we lovingly obey. It does not just come in the atmosphere. First of all, the Kingdom comes to people. When Jesus taught His disciples to pray using the Lord's Prayer outline, part of that prayer was to teach them to say "Your kingdom come" (Matt. 6:10). The next phrase says, "Your will be done on earth [even] as it is in heaven" (Matt. 6:10). Now that is the heart of the Kingdom. It is the will of God being done on Earth the way the will of God is done in Heaven.

One day I was reading the story of the birth of John the Baptist and how the angel Gabriel came to Zacharias. I had read it hundreds of times, so I said, "Lord, what new thing can I get out of this passage of Scripture?" Zacharias had been praying with his wife Elizabeth for a child, and the angel came and said, "Zacharias, your prayer has been heard; you are going to have a son" (see Luke 1:13). Gabriel continued to tell him all the fantastic things that God was going to do with his son. When the angel finished speaking, Zacharias said, "How do I know this will happen?" (See Luke 1:14-18.)

As I was meditating on this, I could almost see the archangel Gabriel's mouth drop. How do I know this is going to happen? The astonished Gabriel replied, "I have just come from the presence of God Almighty! I brought you the rhema word of God, and you are saying, 'How is this going to happen?'" (See Luke 1:19.) Gabriel was absolutely stunned: *I have never heard anybody think or speak like that in heaven. When God speaks, all we think about is implicit, immediate obedience. We don't say "but..." or ask questions. We just obey with the speed of light.*

That is what it means for God's will to be done on Earth as it is in Heaven. It never occurs to angels to question, qualify, or delay the will of God. They have only one ambition and that is to immediately and perfectly fulfill the Word of God. That is the first requirement of the mustard seed. You have to answer this question: "Can I say that my heart's desire, the longing of my heart, is to do God's will and for His will to be done in my life the way it is done in Heaven?" This is, in fact, the first stage of development in Kingdom rule.

STAGE 1: KINGDOM IN YOU

Before I even admitted there was a God, I knew that if there was a God who had created all things, then He had the right to rule over my life. That was never a problem for me, even when I was not a Christian. Therefore, once I came to Christ, I knew the kind of life I had to live. Though I confess that although I knew I had to live that way, I wasn't sure I wanted to. It took me another seven or eight years to come to the place of Matthew 6:33 where Jesus says, "But seek first the kingdom of God and His righteousness, and all these things shall be added to you" (Matt. 6:33). I was keen to make money, to have success, and to live the good life.

After seven or eight years, I came to the place where I saw it. I saw that we are to seek the rule of God over our lives as a hungry man seeks food or a thirsty woman seeks water. It isn't a passive attitude; it is a craving desire. I realized that the worst thing that could possibly happen to me was to miss God's will for my life. There came into me a craving desire to seek the rule, or the government of the Kingdom of God in my life long before I sought material things, fun, success, or even human relationships.

When you really put this first, everything else comes to you without even trying. If you seek first the Kingdom of God, all these other things will be yours as well. Either God is trustworthy or you are going to make an awful crash of your life. He will make you climb out on a limb, but what a faithful God He is when you do!

STAGE 2: KINGDOM IN YOUR FAMILY

After the Kingdom comes to us personally, we have to see to it that the Kingdom comes to our family. When the Kingdom comes into your home, the peace, the joy, and the righteousness of the Kingdom also come to your home.

STAGE 3: KINGDOM IN YOUR CHURCH

Next, the Kingdom has to come to the Church. God's will must be done in the Church the way His will is done in Heaven. If He says something, that is the end of all discussion—just do it. You can gnash your teeth, kick the walls, protest...God is not bothered. He doesn't take any notice of childish tantrums. The most successful life you can live is to fulfill God's will for your life. If God created you to be one of these wonderful serving people who polishes the chairs, lines them up, and looks after the flowers, and you do that your entire life, then you are one hundred percent successful. When you get to Heaven, you will have the same reward as a successful apostle. If you are standing beside an unfaithful apostle, you will have a bigger reward than he will. God rewards faithfulness not prominence. You cannot do more than do God's will. If we get a company of people who are living Kingdom in the church, then the power of that Kingdom is absolutely invincible.

STAGE 4: A PROPERLY-STRUCTURED KINGDOM CHURCH

The next stage is a Kingdom church that is properly structured and understands the basic laws and principles of the Kingdom. A church that can function perfectly in corporeity is a church that can go to war against the kingdom of darkness and absolutely destroy it in the name of Jesus.

The first element of the mustard seed of God is that it is of the Kingdom. The mustard seed of God will begin in you and grow exponentially outward impacting all of society.

THE SEED MUST BE ABLE TO MOVE MOUNTAINS

Look again at Matthew 17. I want to show you the other fundamental dimension of this mustard seed. To set the scene read Luke 9. Jesus sent out the twelve apostles, and for the first time they were moving in the power of the Kingdom. They were casting out demons, healing the sick, and seeing the power of the Kingdom being given to them in advance. Jesus went up on the mount of transfiguration, and Peter, James, and John saw the power and wonder of His glory. These twelve men were on a roll of faith. It was at this point, in the midst of such success, that they came across this demonized boy and were unable to cast the demon out of him. (See Luke 9:1-2;37-40.)

Personally, I believe that one of the prince demons who ruled over Jerusalem saw what was going on. He saw that the Son of God and His twelve apostles were beginning to destroy his kingdom, and he decided to do something about it. The prince demon came himself down and occupied the little boy that we read about in Matthew 17. The disciples had been trying to cast out the demon, and when they were unable, their faith began to trickle away (see Matt. 17:14-20). Be assured, once you start to become effective, once the mustard seed starts to sprout, the devil will come, and he will oppose you. He will come as a personal demonic mountain and drop right on top of your budding tree in an attempt to crush it and stop it from growing.

If you are going to see the mustard seed grow into a tree, then you have to know how to move mountains. This prince demon came himself and withstood the apostles. He was like a great demonic mountain, and he said, "I am not going to move!" When the disciples said, "Come out in the name of Jesus!" nothing happened, and their faith began to fail. If Jesus had not come on the scene, then that would have been the end of their power ministry.

Maybe this has happened to you. You saw the Kingdom and were thrilled with it. You saw some success over the demonic powers, but then a more powerful demon came and dropped a mountain right on top of you. It could be a desperate illness that you cannot shift, a close relationship that was tragically broken, the impossibility of finding new facilities, or maybe you have been attacked in your finances. Whatever it is, there is a mountain in the way, and no matter how hard you try, you can't shift this thing.

When satan drops a mountain in the way, again and again Christians back off, and the devil remains secure. They are left with a little, slightly sprouting mustard seed that never becomes a great tree. It never grows into a tree because demonic opposition has stopped it, and they do not know how to move the mountain out of the way.

The disciples came to Jesus and said, "Why couldn't we cast it out?" (see Matt. 17:19). Jesus said, "It is because of your unbelief. This particular kind doesn't go out except by prayer and fasting" (see Matt. 17:20-21). Now notice this, Jesus did not go up into the mountain for a three day fast before He dealt with this particular demon. Jesus lived a life of prayer and fasting that brought Him into a permanent place of power, faith, and authority so that He was always ready to deal with the mountain. A life of prayer and fasting brings you to a certain kind of authority and to a certain kind of power. As long as you maintain this life, you are a permanent threat to the devil. This is perhaps the most essential quality of those with mustard seed faith. If the church is going to grow into a great tree, then it must learn the kind of faith that can move mountains.

I have often heard this taught, and probably once taught it myself, "*If only you had a little bit of faith like a little mustard seed, then you could say to this mountain….*" That is not what we are being taught here. Mustard seed faith is great faith and a very special kind of faith that can look at five people or a thousand people and say, "In the name of

Jesus, you will grow into a great tree." Once you start to prophesy and the mustard seed begins to grow, you have to be ready to move mountains.

Many years ago, a young Argentinean man named Omar Cabrera went to a little Bible college that consisted of thirty people who gathered in a little building somewhere in Argentina. It was full of problems and all sorts of unrighteous things, but this man had a heart for God. He was just a young man, probably about twenty years of age or so. He would go out into the fields to pray. One day he was out there for so long that they shut the Bible College up and left him out in the field not realizing he was still there. While he was praying in the field, the angel of the Lord came to him. He was absolutely terrified by the awesome presence, and he ran to the college and hammered on the door crying, "Let me in! Let me in!" They all woke up, opened the door, and as he went into the college the angel, now invisible, followed him in.

The college was suddenly filled with the awesome glory of God. The students fell out of bed and rushed down into the chapel. For several weeks they had no lectures. They were just continuously in the presence of God. Incredible prophecies were written in different tongues, not just their native language. They wrote prophecies on the blackboard in languages they had never learned naturally. They wrote prophetic utterances about world events that are being fulfilled even to this day.

Decades later, my son-in-law, Gordon Hickson, met this man and his son. This man had become a terror to the devil. At that point Omar Cabrera had been to eighty cities in Argentina. He would rent a motel room, stay in the room, and pray. He would confront the demonic principality that ruled that region or city, get hold of these demonic mountains, and say, "In the name of Jesus, move!"

On two occasions, the prince demon that ruled a particular region actually manifested himself to this man and tried to bargain with him and to settle "out of court." Omar Cabrera replied, "No, you go. I don't need to bargain. Jesus Christ is Lord around here." He would conquer the principality, cleanse the heavenly atmosphere, and then go out to preach. In every one of the 80 cities, there is now a church of several thousand. That is mustard seed faith! It knows how to move mountains. It can come against principalities and say, "You are not lord around here. Jesus is Lord around here, and you are the one who is going to move."

CHAPTER 10

THE IMPORTANCE OF CURSING THE FIG TREE

W e find another dimension of mustard seed faith in Matthew 21 and Mark 11 where Jesus curses the fig tree. There is some very significant symbolism in this act that I did not mention earlier. The connection to the mustard seed is found in a similar passage where Jesus told His disciples:

> *If you have faith as a mustard seed, you can say to this*
> *mulberry tree [or sycamore fig], "Be pulled up by the*
> *roots and be planted in the sea," and it would obey you*
> (Luke 17:6).

GOD IS LOOKING FOR FRUIT NOT FIG LEAVES

The cursing of the fig tree was significant. To understand why Jesus did it and what it represents, we have to go to the Book of Genesis. Prior to the Fall, Adam and Eve lived before God without any sense of unworthiness. Genesis 2:25 says that they were naked and were not ashamed. That was not only physical. It meant that their souls and their spirits were an open book. There was nothing to hide. They were completely transparent to each other and to God. There was no impurity, and they felt no condemnation. However, after they disobeyed God, instead of running to meet Him when they heard God coming into the Garden, they went and hid.

What a tragic change of circumstance. Adam and Eve realized they had to appear before Him, and thought, *We can't go like this!* They were conscious of the fact that they were now soiled by sin. They found some fig leaves, sewed an apron, and covered themselves with fig leaves thinking that might make them more acceptable to God. They went into the presence of God with sinful souls hoping that a covering of fig leaves would make them acceptable to God. God looked at the fig leaves and said, "Well, those are not going to do you any good." He removed the apron of fig leaves, took an innocent animal, shed its blood, took the skin, and put it upon them as a covering.

That is a tremendous picture of Calvary and what God was going to do for us in Christ. However, there is more here; the fig leaves are significant. The fig leaves are a consistent type or picture of the external covering of religious activity. Whenever a man feels guilty before God, he covers himself with external religious activity hoping it will make him acceptable to God, but it doesn't. Only the blood makes you acceptable to God. Only the Lamb makes you acceptable. You can be as religious as you like. You can be a Hindu, Buddhist, Moslem, Catholic, Baptist, or Pentecostal. It doesn't matter what variety of fig leaves you choose; they are all unacceptable to God. If you put the external covering on but leave the internal heart filled with sin, there is no acceptance by God.

Go through Scripture and look at every mention of figs and fig trees. It is a fascinating study. The fig tree represents the religious life of God's people. God is looking for fruit, not leaves, and figs are the fruit that God desires to eat.

The fig tree is an interesting tree because it is deciduous, yet after its leaves have fallen in the fall, it actually grows fruit buds on the bare branches. The fruit buds remain and are softened by the harsh winter. When the spring comes and the sap rises, these figs begin to grow, mature, and ripen. Those formed at this time are called the first ripe figs or winter figs. Although smaller, they are especially delicious, and particularly sought after, because they have passed through the harshness of winter. After the winter figs, the leaves come, and then a second crop of figs comes after the leaves. These later figs are called the summer figs because they grow in the warmth of the summer. They grow bigger, but are nowhere near as delicious as the winter figs. This picture in nature teaches us that when we pass through hard trials still loving and adoring the Lord, the taste in God's mouth is absolutely delicious, just like the winter figs.

In Jeremiah 24, Jeremiah is shown two baskets of figs. One contained very good figs, like the first ripe winter figs. The other basket contained very bad figs, so bad you couldn't eat them. The two baskets of figs represent two kinds of people who were living in Jerusalem as God was about to judge the city. The first were going to submit to the will of God even if it meant being taken captive by the Chaldeans. God said, "I am going to love them; I am going to turn their hearts during their captivity, and then they will be devoted to Me." He said, "They will serve Me and have one ambition, which is to do My will" (see Jer. 24:4-7).

The other group was rebellious. They were resistant. They were cursing, swearing, and fighting every prophetic word God brought to them. In the end, they went down into Egypt, ended up as captives, and most were destroyed. This rebelliousness was represented by the bad tasting fig. Submission, especially when it is costly and you do not understand it, is perhaps the most delicious flavor to God. The fig tree represented the religious life of the nation of Israel. The leaves represented the outward manifestation of religion. The fruit represented the inward life that pleases and blesses God.

Scripture tells us what kind of fruit God is after.

Therefore by Him let us continually offer the sacrifice of praise to God, that is, the fruit of our lips... (Hebrews 13:15).

When you praise God when things are tough, it is particularly delicious to Him. When you are going through a harsh winter and say, "I am still going to praise You," He loves that praise. However, if you grumble, complain, get depressed, and then on Sunday put on your best suit, go to church, and just put on a religious facade, all He sees is a bunch of fig leaves.

(for the fruit of the Spirit [or the fruit of light] is in all goodness, righteousness, and truth)... (Ephesians 5:9).

But the fruit of the Spirit is love, joy, peace, longsuffering, kindness, goodness, faithfulness, gentleness, self-control. Against such there is no law (Galatians 5:22-23).

But now having been set free from sin, and having become slaves of God, you have your fruit to holiness, and the end, everlasting life (Romans 6:22).

Being filled with the fruits of righteousness which are by Jesus Christ, to the glory and praise of God (Philippians 1:11).

There are many verses that teach us the kind of fruit God desires, but the most wonderful fruit we can have is to reach lost souls and see them saved.

Jesus said to them, "My food is to do the will of Him who sent Me, and to finish His work. Do you not say, 'There are still four months and then comes the harvest'? Behold, I say to you, lift up your eyes and look at the fields, for they are already white for harvest! And he who reaps receives wages, and gathers fruit for eternal life, that both he who sows and he who reaps may rejoice together (John 4:34-36).

THE PARABLE OF THE FIG TREE

At the end of the third year of His ministry, Jesus came into Judea, which was at that time the most religious nation in the world, and all He could see was a great fig tree. Judea was full of religion but had no fruit.

In the Gospel of Luke, Jesus speaks a parable:

A certain man had a fig tree planted in his vineyard, and he came seeking fruit on it and found none. Then he said to the keeper of his vineyard, "Look, for three years I have come seeking fruit on this fig tree and find none. Cut it down; why does it use up the ground?" But he answered and said to him, "Sir, let it alone this year also, until I dig around it and fertilize it. And if it bears fruit, well. But if not, after that you can cut it down" (Luke 13:6-9).

First, note that it says, "and he came seeking fruit" (Luke 13:6). God is always looking for fruit. Then, the parable gets more specific, "for *three years* I have come seeking fruit *on this fig tree* and find none" (Luke 13:7). Jesus told them this parable at the end of the third year of His ministry. Personally, I believe that it was actually a conversation between the Father and the Son. The Father was saying, *"Look at this great religious fig tree called Judaism. I can't find any fruit on it. Cut it down. Why should it occupy the ground any more?"* To which Jesus replied, *"Oh, Father, give me this year to try to plead with these Pharisees and scribes that they might hear the word of God, repent, and at last produce some fruit. If they won't listen, then we will have to cut it down."* This parable gives us the background for the incident where Jesus cursed the fig tree during His last week of ministry.

CURSING THE FIG TREE

Every day during the last week of Jesus' life and the last six days of His ministry, Jesus would go down into Jerusalem and teach in the temple, where there was an atmosphere of growing hostility. Then, every evening, He would go back to the little village of Bethany, which was about two miles outside of Jerusalem, where He would spend the night with Martha, Mary, and Lazarus.

Jesus would bathe Himself in their affection, be strengthened by their love and practical ministry, and then the next day He would go down again to the temple for another day of hostile conflict with the Pharisees and the scribes. His compassion drove Him to do that day after day, because He did not want them to perish. He was trying to bring them to repentance before the day of judgment. However, instead of coming to repentance or acknowledging Him as Lord, they hardened their hearts, became more and more abusive, and plotted more cunningly how they might kill Him.

Just for one day in that last week, the temple was used for its God intended purpose:

> *And He said to them, "It is written, 'My house shall be called a house of prayer,' but you have made it a 'den of thieves.'" Then the blind and the lame came to Him in the temple, and He healed them. But when the chief priests and scribes saw the wonderful things that He did, and the children crying out in the temple and saying, "Hosanna to the Son of David!" they were indignant and said to Him, "Do You hear what these are saying?" And Jesus said to them, "Yes. Have you never read, 'Out of the mouth of babes and nursing infants You have perfected praise'?"* (Matthew 21:13-16).

Once Jesus had cleaned out the temple of the moneychangers, the lame and the sick came to Him, and He healed them all. People went crazy with praise and worship. They adored Him. They danced and cried, "Hosanna to the Son of David!" But the chief priests and scribes said, "*How dreadful! What an awful thing to happen. For goodness sake, tell them not to behave in this disgusting way. It is ruffling all our fig leaves.*"

Jesus responded, "Have you not read in Scripture that 'Out of the mouths of babes and suckling I have perfected praise?'" (see Ps. 8:2). Psalm 8 actually says, "I have perfected strength." There is tremendous strength in being completely abandoned in praise and worship. Learn that strength. The best way to become strong is to be abandoned in adoration and worship of God with your spirit, your soul, and your body. Do that, and the demonic clouds that are hanging around you will disappear. The depression that is over you, the financial problems, and the sicknesses will vanish away.

For one day, that temple shed its fig leaves and started to function the way that God wanted it to function. However, the religious leaders were appalled, and as soon as Jesus walked out of the place, they put the fig leaves back in place and returned to their dead external religion.

On the sixth day of His final week, Jesus came down to the temple as He had done every day. On the way, He saw a fig tree.

> *And seeing a fig tree by the road, He came to it and found nothing on it but leaves, and said to it, "Let no fruit grow on you ever again." Immediately the fig tree withered away* (Matthew 21:19).

Jesus had been trying all week to change the heart of the Pharisees and scribes. He had gone in and cleaned the temple out to show them what it could be like, but they preferred the leaves to the fruit. When He saw an actual fig tree beside the road, He was reminded of His conversation with His Father. Since it had leaves on it, the tree ought to have had at least the first ripe winter figs, if not the summer figs. Jesus looked under the fig leaves, but there was nothing there. It was a perfect allegorical picture of what was going on in the temple. They had the manifestation of religion but not a bit of fruit. He had given them time. He had gone to the temple and preached the Gospel of the Kingdom with demonstrations of power, but there was still no fruit. He had dug around the fig tree and faithfully fertilized it, and it remained barren. At this point, He said, "No one is going to eat fruit from you any more!" and He cursed the fig tree.

Jesus just spoke to the fig tree. We must have this kind of faith. The words alone, spoken in faith, immediately caused the tree to wither. He cursed the fig tree, and it just shriveled up and died.

> *And Peter, remembering, said to Him, "Rabbi, look! The fig tree which You cursed has withered away." So Jesus answered and said to them, "Have faith in God."* (Mark 11:21–22).

Remember that a better translation of what Jesus said to Peter would be "have God's faith." Don't try to work up faith in yourself because that is not going to be the kind of faith that can curse fig trees. When God's Word comes out of your mouth, empowered by the true faith of God, you can speak to these fig trees, and they will shrivel up and die.

WHAT HAPPENS WHEN THE FIG TREE IS CURSED?

Jesus taught and did the mightiest miracles, signs, and wonders that the world has ever seen for a period of three-and-a-half years. Nevertheless, while He drew massive crowds to watch His performance and hear His teaching, only a few hundred truly became His disciples (see 1 Cor. 15:6). The fig tree stopped people from leaving their religion and coming to Christ. They were held in the bondage of their religion. While that fig tree was alive and flourishing, not even the miracles, teaching, and power of Jesus could loose them. Only when Jesus cursed the fig tree were they set free.

After Jesus cursed the fig tree, the next time the Gospel was preached was by Peter on the Day of Pentecost. Out of the same crowd, three thousand people immediately turned to the Lord. The next time it was five thousand. Suddenly this city, which had previously been in the bondage of this great, strong, life-sucking religious fig tree, came to life. When that fig tree was cursed, the ground, occupied by its massive root structure, became vacant. The mustard seed could now be planted in that vacant ground, grow, and become a great tree that filled the heavens with its power. As a result, thousands in Jerusalem were suddenly freed to come to Christ.

Many people go to a fruitless fig tree church and sit under its leaves every Sunday. They are in the bondage of their religion. They are unable to come out of death into the life of Christ because that fruitless fig tree is sucking the life out of them all the time. However once the fig tree is cursed and dies, they can all go free.

We have the opposition of demonic mountains, and we have the bondage of religious fig trees, and that is why we are not yet seeing a great harvest. There is nothing wrong with our preaching, but we have to move the mountains and curse the fig trees before people can respond. Once we do both of those things, the field that was previously barren will suddenly produce a ripe, fruitful, mighty harvest.

FREE THE NEXT GENERATION

I want to show you one more thing regarding fig trees. We read at the beginning of John's Gospel when Jesus first began His ministry the following words:

> *The following day Jesus wanted to go to Galilee, and He found Philip and said to him, "Follow Me." Now Philip was from Bethsaida, the city of Andrew and Peter. Philip found Nathanael and said to him, "We have found Him of whom Moses in the law, and also the prophets wrote—Jesus of Nazareth, the son of Joseph." And Nathanael said to him, "Can anything good come out of Nazareth?" Philip said to him, "Come and see." Jesus saw Nathanael coming toward Him, and said of him, "Behold, an Israelite indeed, in whom is no deceit!" Nathanael said to Him, "How do You know me?" Jesus answered and said to him, "Before Philip called you, when you were under the fig tree, I saw you"* (John 1:43-48).

There is a whole generation of young people who have grown up under their parents' fig trees. They might be Baptist fig trees, Pentecostal fig trees, Presbyterian fig trees, Lutheran fig trees, and so on. They are sick to death of religion without passion. They have become absolute cynics. Get them out from under the fig tree, let them have one real encounter with the living Lord Jesus, and they will be completely transformed. All Jesus did was move in one simple word of knowledge, and this young man knew that there was a living God, and he was hooked for life.

Even if the old people have learned to survive under these various Christian fig trees, we must curse these trees for the sake of the younger generation. We must free these young people from these fig trees and from their cynicism, unbelief, and doubt. We must bring them into a vital encounter with the living Christ. It is time to move in the gifts of the Spirit and in the power of God, and show them that God is real, relevant, and alive. When we do that, many will follow Him with zeal and power and bring transformation to our cities.

CHAPTER 11

THE SHIELD OF FAITH

If we are going to fight the good fight of faith, we must understand what it means to take up the shield of faith. The goal is to become a warring church that reaps a mighty harvest. The first step in becoming that warring church is learning to defend ourselves with pure golden shields of faith.

In his letter to the church of Ephesus, Paul says,

Above all, taking the shield of faith with which you will be able to quench all the fiery darts of the wicked one (Ephesians 6:16).

Notice the superlatives in this verse. First, you have to do this "above all." Secondly, you will be able to quench "all the fiery darts of the wicked one"—not some of them, but all of them. This means that if we really get hold of this verse, we will live in continuous victory. Whatever the devil throws at us will be neutralized by the shield of faith.

MADE OF PURE GOLD

With that as the primary text, look at First Kings 10. Solomon has completed the temple, the glory of the kingdom has reached unprecedented proportions, and the Queen of Sheba has come to see this incredible kingdom she has been hearing about. She has heard about its power, glory, and magnificence, and she comes to Solomon with a great retinue of servants. When she sees how magnificent the kingdom is, the breath is knocked out of her, and she says, "indeed the half was not told me. Your wisdom and prosperity exceed the fame of which I heard" (1 Kings 10:7).

The kingdom that awed the queen of Sheba was the shadow of a much more glorious reality: the Kingdom of our Lord Jesus Christ. This earthly kingdom, that began during David's reign and went into the early years of Solomon's reign, was the shadow of the Kingdom that was yet to come. The shadow gives us a physical benchmark by which we can measure the glory of the spiritual Kingdom that God is going to establish. It gives us some idea of the glory that God intends for His Kingdom before Jesus can come and consummate it with His second coming. We are told that the glory of that Kingdom is going to cover the Earth as the waters cover the sea (see Hab. 2:14).

God is going to shake nations. There are many mighty things promised in Scripture that have to happen before Jesus can come. Something incredibly powerful and of great proportions is going to have to hit this Earth in order for these Scriptures to be fulfilled. Something spiritual beyond our imagination is going to have to be let loose, and I have the feeling that it is getting wonderfully close.

In First Kings we are given a picture of the kingdom's riches:

The weight of gold that came to Solomon yearly was six hundred and sixty-six talents of gold, besides that from the traveling merchants, from the income of traders, from all the kings of Arabia, and from the governors of the country (1 Kings 10:14–15).

Six hundred and sixty-six talents of gold is an immense sum of money. At today's prices, that would be over $650 million. Yet, that was just the beginning. On top of that were the revenues from "the traveling merchants, from the income of traders, from all the kings of Arabia and from the governors of the country."

From this picture, the first thing we notice is that the financial resources were more than adequate to run the Kingdom. I haven't the slightest desire to drive a gold-plated Cadillac, wear gold suits, and have gold dripping all over me, but I do want adequate resources to advance the Kingdom. The Kingdom should not lack any resources to achieve the purposes of God. If I were given ten million dollars today, I would know what to do with it right away, and I wouldn't spend any of it on myself.

There are demonic spirits sent by the devil to keep believers short financially, to keep them restricted, to keep their finances impaired in order that they may not release the necessary resources into the Kingdom. Financial blessing is not for our personal gain. One of the reasons God cannot release the full weight of finances into the Kingdom is because we have not yet learned how to handle it selflessly. We need to say, "God, I want to learn how to be a faithful steward of the resources that You put into my hand." If God gives me a little and I can't handle it, then He is not going to give me a lot. However, he that is faithful in little will be given much (see Luke 19:11-27). I am praying for multimillionaires to be raised up who will live on two to five percent of their income and put the rest into the Kingdom. I am praying for multimillionaires who will invest in the Kingdom of Heaven rather than using it in this world.

> *And King Solomon made two hundred large shields of hammered gold; six hundred shekels of gold went into each shield. He also made three hundred shields of hammered gold; three minas of gold went into each shield. The king put them in the House of the Forest of Lebanon* (1 Kings 10:16-17).

In Scripture, certain physical things have a consistent spiritual meaning. Gold represents divine nature, and brass represents human nature. When you read about gold in Scripture, it often represents the nature of God. For example, First Peter says,

> *In this you greatly rejoice, though now for a little while, if need be, you have been grieved by various trials, that the genuineness of your faith, being much more precious than gold that perishes, though it is tested by fire, may be found to praise, honor, and glory at the revelation of Jesus Christ* (1 Peter 1:6-7).

The kind of faith that I am talking about in this book is the divine faith that comes from God. It is golden faith. It has passed through the fiery trials and has come out guaranteed as genuine gold. If you are going through some trials, even if the devil is kicking you, behind it all is a sovereign God wanting to bring forth something. He wants to bring forth the pure gold of tried faith.

HAMMERED INTO SHAPE

God does not just want faith; He wants faith He can use. It is quite painful to be hammered and beaten into shape, but that is the only way that faith becomes a golden shield by which we can quench all the fiery darts of the enemy. After being heated in the fire, we must be forged into something usable.

In the great house of glory that King Solomon established, all the walls were lined with golden shields. Each one weighed about fifteen pounds and was worth something like $200,000 U.S. dollars. God will spare no expense to bring forth for Himself a company of people who have come through the fire, been hammered into shape, and are now mighty shields who can destroy and defeat all the fiery darts of the devil.

The early church in many ways carried the glory of Solomon's temple. They had real faith. Peter, Paul, and the other apostles marched through the nations with bright, glistening, golden shields of faith. They went single handed into cities full of demonic darkness. The devil threw everything he could at them, but they were impregnable to the power of the devil because they were invincible in their faith.

Somewhere along the road, we have lost it. The cry of God is to take people to this point of impregnable faith again. However, it is not going to be a fun trip, and He will only take those who are willing. There is going to be pain and cost involved. You cannot have instant faith. The only way to produce pure gold is to take it through the fire. Remember what Jesus said to the church at Laodicea: "Buy of Me gold tried in the fire." He said, "*You say that you are rich, increasing in goods and lacking nothing. You don't know how blind you are or how poor you are. In showing off all your dazzling equipment, your techniques, your facilities and all the other things, you have lost something very precious. You have lost your faith. I urge you to buy of Me real gold. You are going to have to pay a price for this. I can give you salvation for free, but I cannot give you golden faith for free. It is going to cost you something."* (See Revelation 3:17-18.)

D.L. Moody was mightily used during the great evangelical awakening. He influenced thousands of young people to go to the nations. Moody went into foreign countries around the world and stormed the bastions of demonic darkness. Often missionaries to these countries lived between two and four years before they were either killed by the native people or died of various diseases. The average life expectancy was between three-and-a-half and four years, but that did not stop them from going; they went to die. I don't mean they looked for death, but to them it was a reasonable price to pay in order to see the Kingdom come.

God released many in those days who shook the world. To this day, we are reaping the benefits of the price they paid. However, the bank accounts are running short. In fact, many of them are in the red, and God is saying, "Who is going to pay the price?" They invested in the bank of Heaven, and we have been living in the good of their investments. Nevertheless, I tell you, we are running into bankruptcy, and a new generation has to pay a new price in order to release a new power that will destroy the works of darkness.

The Church in that time was glorious. The whole world was glistening with these marvelous hammered, beaten, golden shields. The Church was amazingly strong with a mighty faith. It was invincible. Laying down their lives was a reasonable service. It was not anything special. It was normal.

The devil had no way around such a committed people. There was no way he could defeat them because they put up their shields of faith and said, "You can kill me, but if you do, you are going to pay for it." Missions around the world experienced mighty revivals because of the blood of the martyrs.

I don't know whether you are going to lay your life down physically, but you can lay your life down just as realistically by saying, "God, I am really going to live for You." You might have to lower your standard of living or relocate to a needy area of the city. That is reasonable service. Somehow, it seems reasonable in a foreign country, but in your own country you say, "I can't do that!" If we would invade all areas of our society with men and women marching in the glistening power of these mighty, invincible shields of faith, nothing could stop us.

Second Chronicles 9 tells the same story. By Second Chronicles 12 Solomon had died, and his son Rehoboam had come to the throne. Then it says in verse 2:

And it happened in the fifth year of King Rehoboam that Shishak king of Egypt came up against Jerusalem, because they had transgressed against the Lord, with twelve hundred chariots, sixty thousand horsemen, and people without number who came with him out of Egypt—the Lubim and the Sukkiim and the Ethiopians. And he took the fortified cities of Judah and came to Jerusalem (2 Chronicles 12:2-4).

Then a prophet came and said,

You have forsaken Me, and therefore I also have left you in the hand of Shishak (2 Chronicles 12:5).

Beginning in verse 9, we read the sad consequences of sin:

So Shishak king of Egypt came up against Jerusalem, and took away the treasures of the house of the Lord and the treasures of the king's house; he took everything. He also carried away the gold shields which Solomon had made. Then King Rehoboam made bronze shields in their place, and committed them to the hands of the captains of the guard, who guarded the doorway of the king's house. And whenever the king entered the house of the Lord, the guard would go and bring them out; then they would take them back into the guardroom (2 Chronicles 9-11).

Egypt represents the world, and the prince of this world is satan. Through worldliness, he was able to come and take away the golden shields of the people of God. Because worldliness has invaded the Church, we have lost our faith.

Rehoboam made new shields out of bronze, which looks a bit like gold as long as you don't look at it too carefully. Bronze in Scripture stands for human nature, which stands in the place of divine nature. Moses was told by God to make a bronze serpent and hang it on the tree. Everyone who looked at the bronze serpent was saved from their snakebite. That is a tremendous picture of God crucifying the Adamic human nature in Christ Jesus. If we are willing to have our human nature crucified with Christ, then the disease of sin stops dead and we are delivered from the bite of the serpent. This beautiful imagery runs consistently throughout Scripture.

Rehoboam, aware that the golden shields had been taken away, went and made some bronze shields. Whenever the king came into the meeting place, they took these bronze shields out of the guardroom and paraded them around. They made all sorts of warlike noises while the king was there. Once the king left, they put them back in the guardroom because they were afraid they might be stolen.

This is a picture of us today. When we are in a time of corporate praise and worship, we bring out our bronze shields and say, "Yes, Jesus is Lord! We are going to take the Kingdom for God!" We wave our bronze shields around, but once the meeting is over, we put them away and don't think about spiritual battles again until next week. It is very easy to learn the song of Zion without ever getting into the battle of Zion.

Someone, I believe it was A. W. Tozer, once said, "There are many Christians who are fiercely ready, but they never quite get into the fight." We put on the shield, but it is not a real golden shield; it is a bronze shield. It looks impressive at a distance. On a Sunday morning, we can go through a charade of being a soldier of Christ, but to actually go out to war and fight the devil, no thanks! Every time the king comes into the temple, we make warlike noises, and when he goes away, we put away our instruments of war.

We have lost our golden shields and made for ourselves counterfeit bronze shields. They look like faith until they are put to the test. We are prepared to make declarations of faith until the devil comes against us and claims the right to test our faith. Once he is permitted to try our faith, most of us quit and get out of the battle. We are not serious about wanting to wage war.

GREAT WEAPON OF CORPORATE FAITH

The early church had real faith. At the gate called Beautiful in Acts 3 Peter said:

And His name, through faith in His name, has made this man strong, whom you see and know. Yes, the faith which comes through Him has given him this perfect soundness in the presence of you all (Acts 3:16).

In Acts 6, when the disciples picked seven people to have charge of the daily distribution of the food to the needy people, we read that

...they chose Stephen, a man full of faith and the Holy Spirit (Acts 6:5).

He wasn't a famous international speaker; he was just a guy who spent most of his time preparing meals for the needy people in town. Nevertheless, on the side, he effectively warred against the devil.

And Stephen, full of faith and power, did great wonders and signs among the people (Acts 6:8).

He was doing mighty works and miracles, but no one considered this extraordinary because the entire church was like that. Philip was a deacon who went down to Samaria, evangelized Syria, and amazed the place with signs and wonders. They had something in that generation that we have not recovered.

The Book of Ephesians was written to prepare the church for a time of heightened warfare. However, you cannot get to chapter 6 without going through the preparation of chapters 1-5. Neither can we be strong in our corporeity until we are strong individually.

Joshua 23:10 says,

One man of you shall chase a thousand, for the Lord your God is He who fights for you, as He promised you (Joshua 23:10).

We must be strong individually because our corporate strength will always be weakened by the weakest member of the team. Corporate faith is a multiplication of the individual faith. As individuals, you and I have to learn how to chase a thousand so that we will have something to multiply when we come together. If a group of people who are chasing nothing come together, zero multiplied by one hundred is still zero. Coming together doesn't make someone who has nothing any more powerful.

It is necessary for us to be strong individually, but the purpose is not to have spiritual supermen and women who fly around on their own. The major purpose for being strong as individuals is what we can do when we come together as the Body of Christ. David's mighty men could do incredible feats individually, but they were willing to lay down their individual agendas to become the great army of the Lord.

In Leviticus 26 God gives the Israelites all kinds of promises, but those promises were conditional upon verse 3. God tells them,

If you walk in My statutes and keep My commandments, and perform them, then I will... (Leviticus 26:3-4).

God continues to list the blessings that would follow if they as a community would walk in His statues and keep His commands. In verse seven He promises,

You will chase your enemies, and they shall fall by the sword before you. Five of you shall chase a hundred, and a hundred of you shall put ten thousand to flight; your enemies shall fall by the sword before you. For I will look on you favorably and make you fruitful, multiply you and confirm My covenant with you (Leviticus 26:7-9).

The real power of the Church is found in corporeity. The good fight of faith is not the place for lone rangers to go out and do things on their own. That is not part of God's concept of how the Body of Christ is supposed to fight. If we are strong individually, then we will be able to multiply our individual strengths when we come together. Together 5 will chase 100, and 100 will chase 10,000. Our power grows exponentially as we come together in unity and in corporate obedience.

The responsibility for developing corporate faith does not rest on any one person. If I have a personal life of faith but am in a church that is full of unbelief, then my faith may never triumph over the unbelief of the Body. We have a corporate responsibility to come to faith. In the early church when the apostles went out, mighty signs and wonders followed them, not simply because of who they were individually but because of the Church that was behind them. They went out as the expression of the faith of the whole Body. If I had a mighty strong index finger, but the rest of my body was wasted away with muscle disease, what could I actually do? I could wave my big finger, but what could that do? However, if that muscular finger is part of a mighty muscular body, then that whole body can do mighty exploits and powerful things.

We have a corporate responsibility to come to faith. We have a corporate responsibility to pass through the fire and come out the other side with hundreds of mighty golden shields of faith. Whatever the devil throws at us, we need to go back at him with even greater aggression, above all taking the shield of faith with which we can quench all the fiery darts of the devil (see Eph. 6:16).

Lord, I want to buy this gold of You. Take me through the fire and purify my faith. I want a shield of faith that is made of pure gold. Burn away what is left of my human nature and pour into me Your divine nature. Take my life, Lord. As the saints of old, I choose to count that as my reasonable service. Where I am weak, make me strong.

Divinely connect me with others of like faith. As I go out, I want to be a representative of a Body of believers who have become a great weapon of corporate faith. Grow my church, my community, my city, my nation into a corporate Body that is full of Your great faith. May we line the nation with bright, beautiful, golden shields of faith. Enable us to stand together as one, locking our shields together so that our strength may be multiplied and every wicked scheme of the evil one will be extinguished.

Bind us together in love and in the unity of the Spirit. May we go out together in a beautiful, strong, corporate expression of faith. Give us a corporate faith that breaks down every stronghold and principality, moves in signs and wonders, and forcefully advances the Kingdom of God. Do it, Lord, in the mighty name of Jesus Christ.

CHAPTER 12

MOVING FROM FAITH TO FAITH

W e have to keep coming to new levels of faith. In the good fight of faith, we must move progressively forward. We cannot get to one level and stagnate there; we must push forward in order to keep winning our battles against the evil one and see the Kingdom of God established here on Earth. Scripture repeatedly says that the righteous must live by His faith and clearly teaches a progression of faith. Romans 1 tells us that we move from faith to faith:

> *So, as much as is in me, I am ready to preach the gospel to you who are in Rome also. For I am not ashamed of the gospel of Christ: for it is the power of God to salvation for everyone who believes, for the Jew first, and also for the Greek. For in it the righteousness of God is revealed **from faith to faith**: as it is written, "The just shall live by faith"* (Romans 1:15-17).

The more we use our faith, the more God will give us. He will present us with bigger and bigger situations that require more and more faith. He will use situations like physical sickness, financial lack, or some other problem to develop our faith. He may tell us to step out and do something that we have never done before.

In this chapter, I am going to mention three distinct levels of faith that we must progress through and give us some specific steps to take in order to go from one level to the next. The principles themselves have been mentioned previously, but I want to emphasize the progression.

LEVEL 1: DEFENSIVE FAITH

First, there is *defensive faith.* If you do not have your defensive faith intact, then there is no point in bothering about the others. Until you can defend yourself, it is not wise to go to war because you are going to be defeated. Before anything else, you have to learn the faith that is produced through fiery trial. You have to get to the place where no matter what the devil throws at you, you are invincible to his attack and can defend yourself.

Before there is a day of glorious breakthrough, there will be an evil day of trial and testing. However, you can stand in the evil day. The main weapon of your defense is holding onto the Word of God by faith when you are going through tough trials.

> *Put on the whole armor of God that you may be able to stand against the wiles of the devil, for we do not wrestle against flesh and blood, but against principalities, against powers, against the rulers of the darkness of this age, against spiritual host of wickedness in the heavenly places* (Ephesians 6:11-12).

You have to be able to put in place the kind of faith that can stand in the evil day.

LEVEL 2: PRAYING FAITH THAT OBTAINS

The second level is learning how to use *praying faith effectively.* In Luke 11:5, Jesus tells the story of the man who goes to his friend at midnight and asks him for three loaves because he has a friend in need, and he has nothing to set before him. He knocks on the door, and the friend says, "Go away! It is too late now; we have all gone to bed." But, the man keeps hammering and hammering, and finally his friend gets up and gives him everything he needs (see Luke 11:5-8). The goal in learning praying faith is to get to the level of faith where you can legally and righteously call down all you need to meet your friend's need.

Jesus wants us to learn the power of importunate prayer. Persistent prayer obtains things. At this point, you are not yet in real spiritual warfare, but you are learning something of the kind of faith that demands persistence. You are learning to hold onto your faith no matter what circumstances look like, what others say, or how ridiculous you look. This principle of importunate prayer applies to the whole realm of obtaining things through faith, not just for you, but persisting in prayer and obtaining things for others as well.

When the children of Israel were in the wilderness they had many miracles of provision: they had the water come miraculously out of the rock, God sent them manna every day, the quails were wonderfully provided for them, their clothes never got old, and their shoes never wore out. You have the right to ask God for your essential needs and for the needs of those around you, but you must know how. Moses did not call forth water from the rock and manna from the heavens sufficient just for himself and his immediate family.

All of Israel benefited from his faith. We must come to the place where we know how to obtain from God, not for our own selfish greed, but for our essential needs and the needs of others.

The Israelites went through the wilderness having everything necessary provided for them, but they were still in the wilderness not the promised land. The wilderness is part of God's training ground. Learning the kind of faith that obtains everything you need often requires going through the wilderness where you are completely dependent on God alone for your provision. It is a training ground that is not as prevalent in some countries as in others. However, even in plush America, God can structure your circumstances so that you are left with God as your only means of supply. It is scary, but it is a great place to be. Boot camp is hard, but it prepares you for war. Being in a place where you are completely dependent on God for your supply is not a disaster. It is a blessing if you handle it with the right kind of faith. When you see God miraculously provide for you, you will see that the God of the great faith-filled missionaries of the past is also your God. He will supply your needs just as He supplied theirs.

Leaning completely on God's provision was an essential part of my training, and I still live that way today. Eileen and I lived in India without the support of a mission agency for thirteen years. There were times when I sweated some, but we never wrote a begging letter or made our needs known, and we saw God supply. We still do.

You are allowed to be tried. The devil will challenge you just as he did Job. When God provides for you, the devil says to Him, "Oh, he is only faithful because You are blessing him" (see Job 1:10-11). God will allow the provision to be withdrawn for a time in order to see how you behave with your faith. Are you faithful when God's provision, protection, and blessings are taken away?

If we seek first the Kingdom of God and His righteousness, He promises us that all these other things will be ours as well (see Matt. 6:33). I am not talking mere theory. I have been through the trials, and I can honestly say that God has abundantly provided for me, for my family, and for the work for which I am responsible. I have come out the other side with a faith intact, knowing the absolute reliability of my God. As it is, I am a free man. I can go anywhere and live anywhere and not worry about financial supply because I know my God will provide.

My wife and I are never concerned about whether we can afford something; we are only concerned about whether it is the will of God or not. Praying faith that obtains things from God requires responsibility and stewardship. I don't hesitate to buy things if God has sanctioned them, but I dare not buy things that God has not sanctioned, even if I have the money. I have never bought a thing on credit in my life. If God can't pay for it, I don't want it.

The wilderness is part of God's training, but it is not the promised land. Do not be content to waste your life wandering around the desert just because your needs are being met and you are afraid of going to war.

LEVEL 3: WARRING FAITH

Having a persistent praying faith that obtains things from God is a step on the way to the third kind of faith, which is the faith that can and will go to war. Once you have learned to obtain things from God through persistent prayer, you must be ready to engage in warfare.

The third level of faith is *warring faith*. In Luke 18, the importunate widow said to the judge, "Avenge me of my adversary." Jesus said in verse 1 that He taught this parable so that men and women might learn to pray and not to faint (see Luke 18:1). When you start to petition in the realm of spiritual warfare, the temptation to faint is considerable because all the fury of hell will be let loose against you. The devil will do his utmost to stop you from pressing home the case.

In that parable you have the judge, you have the defendant, and you have the prosecution. The judge is God, the defendant is satan, and the prosecution is any man or woman, however small and insignificant, who has the courage and faith to demand that the victory of Calvary be implemented and practiced in their society. We are not winning a battle; we are enforcing a victory that has already been won.

The first battle is a legal battle, not a military engagement. Before we wage war on a battlefield, we do battle in court. We go into the heavenly courtroom with the cast-iron faith of what Jesus did at Calvary and what the Word of God says.

Come into the courtroom and say,

Father, we want You to prosecute the devil in our city. He is messing up the lives of thousands of children; little babies are being murdered by abortion; and adultery and abuse are destroying people's lives. So, Father, will You please avenge us of the adversary who is causing all of this.

I can assure you that the heart of God is one hundred percent with you. However, He is a righteous God, and He has to allow satan to plead his case.

In this dispensation, the devil has a right to use the agencies of men and women in the continuation of his kingdom. When we challenge that, he will start the counterattack. That is where the battle is going to go first, and that is where you have to be prepared to fight.

If a man says, "God, will You send twenty legions of angels and drive the demons out for us?" He says, "Yes, I will, but first the devil wants to raise an objection. I have to hear the devil's case and allow him to make every legal protest he can." If you stay pleading your case, eventually the devil will run out of excuses, his defenses will come to an end, and then God can righteously give you the judgment.

Jesus said, "Men ought always to pray and not to faint" (Luke 18:1 KJV), but, unfortunately, we do faint, and we do give up. God needs men and women who will stand. In Luke 18:1-8, He says at the end, "when the Son of Man comes, will He really find faith on the earth?" (see Luke 18:8). He is looking for someone with the kind of warring faith that will stay in there until the heavenly verdict is given.

Once the legal case has been won, God can release twelve legions of angels to drive every demon out of town. But until you have won the legal case, you are not going to win military battles. I am not against demonstration, I am not against the physical manifestation of our displeasure over what is going on in the Earth, but until we have legions of angels backing us outside those abortion clinics, we are not really going to change things. If we go to war with legions of angels driving the demons out before us, the whole climate will change.

We may say the same things and do the same things, but after we win the legal battle, there is a mighty spiritual power behind it. On Sunday morning the preacher will ask, "Who wants Jesus?" and thousands of people will flock to the front to get saved. It will happen, not because he has suddenly become an incredible preacher, but because a widow woman prayed, and as a result every demon has been driven out, and the place is filled with defending angels. That is warring faith.

STEPS FOR MOVING TO THE NEXT LEVEL

How does faith grow in us? How does it develop? Faith is not imparted overnight. There are certain specific things that bring us to faith and move us from one level of faith to the next.

NUMBER 1: BECOME DESPERATE

Rachel cried out, "Give me children, or else I die!" (Gen. 30:1). The Canaanite woman was so desperate to see her daughter healed that she walked right through every obstacle Jesus put in her way. Desperation propels us forward when we might otherwise be inhibited by people's opinions or theological issues.

When I used to travel around India with my wife and our children, when we got sick, we couldn't just go down the street to the local family practitioner. We knew that if God did not act, we were finished. We experienced numerous miraculous healings because we prayed so desperately. God was our only hope.

One day after we had been living in America for several years, my wife said, "Pray for me I have a terrible headache." I find it so much more difficult to pray in faith in America than I did in India because I know we can always go to the doctor if it doesn't work. I told her, "I wish we were in the middle of Nepal."

Cry to God for a new desperation over the state of this nation, over the state of the world. *God, impart to me Your passion. I want to share Your heart. I want to become desperate over these days.* I believe that desperate prayer is the seed of faith. Jesus said "Blessed are those that hunger and thirst after righteousness, for they shall be filled" (Matt. 5:6).

NUMBER 2: BECOME DEPENDENT

Faith comes from God. Real faith, this golden shield of faith, is a gift. It comes right out of God's Spirit into our spirit. We have to recognize our complete and utter dependency on Him. We have to say, "*God, there is no way that I can produce faith on my own; I need You to impart Your faith. I am desperate for an impartation of Your faith. I am adamantly cast upon You. I have nothing to set before the people. There is nothing I can do to relieve the demonic darkness. I am weak and helpless, but God, I am looking to You for Your supply.*"

Jesus said, "Blessed are the poor in spirit, for theirs is the kingdom of heaven" (Matt. 5:3). As long as I think I am rich, I have nothing. Acknowledge an utter poverty in yourself, and look to God to meet your need. Be completely dependent on Him.

NUMBER 3: PUT AWAY UNBELIEF

Unbelief has to go. The Bible says, "Blessed are those who mourn" (Matt. 5:4), and the thing I mourn about most is the unbelief that hinders the faith of God. I have come to hate unbelief in my own heart more than I can possibly describe to you. We must rebuke the spirit of unbelief that works contrary to faith and silence every voice of unbelief that tries to negate the power of God.

NUMBER 4: BE READY TO BE PERSUADED BY THE WORD OF GOD

Put away rational, earthly, intellectual thinking that hinders childlike faith. Read the Word of God with the faith of a child who does not question or doubt anything his or her Father says.

NUMBER 5: LEARN TO HEAR

So then faith comes by hearing, and hearing by the word of God (Romans 10:17).

If you can't hear God, then there is nothing for your faith to grab hold of. Faith cannot operate in a vaccum without the Word of God being there. It is absolutely paramount that you and I are soaked and saturated with the Word of

God. Furthermore, we must hear God speak His specific word to us. Romans 10:17 does not say, faith comes by reading the Word of God; faith comes by hearing the Word of God. We must hear the specific word of God spoken to our spirit by His Spirit.

NUMBER 6: FAITH WORKS BY LOVE

For in Christ Jesus neither circumcision nor uncircumcision avails anything, but faith working through love (Galatians 5:6).

If I want to receive God's faith, I have to be taken up with His love. I have to know I am loved by Him. I have to be caught up to Him. God and I have to become lovers. That was the cry of Jesus to the Ephesian church, "You have lost your first love" (see Rev. 2:4).

NUMBER 7: BE HUMBLE AND TEACHABLE

Jesus said to His disciples,

Blessed are the meek, for they shall inherit the earth (Matthew 5:5).

Jesus also said the following to the Pharisees and the scribes:

How can you believe, who receive honor from one another...? (John 5:44).

That is the problem with much of our leadership in this land. How can you believe, how can you move in faith, when you seek and receive honor from one another? We have to humble ourselves so we are teachable. Status and recognition from our peers cannot be our motivation or affirmation. Pride drives us to do things in our own strength and take credit that does not belong to us. Humility recognizes that everything we do is for God and is utterly dependent on God.

NUMBER 8: EXERCISE THE FAITH YOU HAVE

It says in James chapter 2 that faith without works is dead (see Jam. 2:26). You have to get up and attempt to do works of faith. If you make a mistake, you make a mistake. So what? Someone said that if you have never made a mistake, you have never made anything. Aim at nothing, and you are sure to hit it. When you make mistakes, be teachable, be honest, and be ready to be corrected.

I have learned from my mistakes. In fact, I have made so many mistakes that I am now considered wise! In the Scriptures, God never rebuked anyone who stepped out in faith with a goal. Think of Caleb and Caleb's daughter. Think of Peter who said, "Lord, bid me to come and walk with You on the water." How did Jesus respond to such a request? He simply said, "Come." The fact that Peter sank didn't bother Jesus: *Well, you shouldn't have let your faith wobble.* God will put up with an enormous amount from those who are prepared to step out and try to do things for Him. If you make mistakes, well, make them, but learn on the way. Get up again and have another go!

NUMBER 9: MAINTAIN YOUR GOOD CONFESSION

We have seen Paul's three instructions to Timothy in First Timothy 6:12-14:

1. Fight the good fight of faith

2. Lay hold on the eternal life, to which you were also called

3. Maintain the good confession before many witnesses

In this third instruction, Paul is saying, *Timothy, you've got to keep that good confession. You've got to keep your mouth speaking faith even when your circumstances appear to be totally contrary to what you are saying. Remember the good confession that Jesus made before Pontius Pilate. That is to be the motivation for you to keep a good confession.*

Abraham made a few stops along his way to faith. Twice he presented Sarah as his sister rather than his wife because he was afraid (see Gen. 12:10-13; 20:1-3). They both initially laughed in unbelief at God's outrageous promise to them (see Gen. 17:17; 18:10-13). Yet they were persuadable. Faced with the commandment to kill his own son, Abraham clung to the faith he had. He reasoned with himself against unbelief. He chose to believe God's promise even as he was preparing to kill his son—and therefore concluded that God would have to raise him from the dead. He maintained his good confession of faith (see Gen. 22). By the time Abraham arrived in the promised land, he realized that the promise of God was for so much more than what he had initially believed. He came to faith that his inheritance was now to inherit the whole Earth.

If you go through the Gospels, Peter had several attempts to become a man of faith with varying success. The most spectacular thing he had done prior to the resurrection was to walk on the water temporarily. The other disciples did not even try, but even Peter after a few steps looked at the total ridiculousness and the rational impossibility of what he was doing and said, "I can't be doing this!" Once he began to think that way, down he went. (See Matthew 14:25-32.)

Peter had tried and tried to become a man of faith, just by watching Jesus, with little sprinklings of success and with lots of disappointments. He wasn't where he wanted to be, and Jesus knew that. That could be you. Maybe you've tried a few things, and if you compared your successes to your failures, you might be a bit like Peter. Peter was still trying to do things by his own abilities and his own faith. Jesus said, "Peter, have God's faith."

When Jesus was arrested in the Garden, Peter failed Jesus. He was as scared, broken, and hopeless as anyone could be. However, with Jesus, Peter made a great recovery; he came back, received the Holy Spirit, received God's faith, and changed the world.

You may be like Peter and have tried and failed. You may be like Paul and have been fighting for the other side. You may have never stepped into the ring, completely unaware that a fight was being fought. It makes no difference to God. Whatever your past, whatever your present, maintain your good confession. If you will receive His faith, He can transform you and use you mightily.

Until God closes the door of salvation to humankind, God must work through the agency of men and women. Paul counted the cost and gladly paid the price. While he suffered tremendously, he never gave up his faith, and, as a result, he saw amazing victories. Having been through the full gamut of human experience, he learned the secret to being content in any and every circumstance. Desiring to pass on what he had learned, he wrote to his dearly beloved son in the faith, Timothy. He told him to fight the good fight of faith, lay hold on the eternal life to which he was also called, and maintain the good confession he made in front of many witnesses.

We must do the same. It is a fight, but if we will persevere to the end, if we will finish the race, we will find it to be a very "good" fight indeed. The victory has already been won. The future is clear. Which side of the fence will you be on? In Revelation, the Lord makes seven promises to those who overcome. How do we overcome? We overcome by our faith.

> *For everyone born of God overcomes the world. This is the victory that has overcome the world, even our faith* (1 John 5:4 NIV).

At the end of your life, may you be able to say as Paul did:

> *I have fought the good fight, I have finished the race, I have kept the faith* (2 Timothy 4:7).

I encourage you to mark your completion of this book with a new commitment to God and a bold declaration of faith. You may even want to take communion. Count the cost, and make it as personal as you can. Listen to the Spirit as He guides you in what specific things to pray and declare by faith.

> *Lord, I'm desperate for Your faith. Forgive me for my unbelief. I commit to You that from this day on, I will not focus on my failures, my circumstances, what seems rational, or what others*

say, but I commit to listen to You alone. I will immediately obey what You tell me to do. I will step out in childlike faith on Your Word.

I rebuke the spirit of unbelief! I refuse to listen to the lies of the enemy anymore and declare that not one negative word of unbelief will pass through my lips. I yield myself, my life, my spirit to You, Lord. Infuse me with Your faith, Your heart, and Your Word so that the words of my mouth and the meditations of my heart are pleasing to You.

Right now, I lay hold of the eternal life to which You have called me. Open the eyes of my heart so that I can see the things that are unseen more clearly than the things that are seen. I step into eternity and grab hold of all that You have promised me. I declare that I am a new creation in Christ. I am pure, holy, and have the righteousness of Christ. I curse the fig tree and declare that never again will I clothe myself with fig leaves. I am a mighty warrior of faith, and I stand against the enemy with my golden shield of faith.

I will fight the good fight of faith, no matter what it costs me. I will finish the race, no matter how many times I fall. I will keep the faith, no matter who stands against me. Remembering Jesus' good confession before Pontius Pilate, I will maintain my good confession of faith even if I must carry it to my grave.

I will overcome the world with my faith. I will...because I believe and trust in the Lord Jesus Christ. I believe in the God who is.

In the name of the Lord Jesus Christ,

Amen.

Additional copies of this book and other book titles from DESTINY IMAGE are available at your local bookstore.

Call toll-free: 1-800-722-6774.

Send a request for a catalog to:

Destiny Image® Publishers, Inc.
P.O. Box 310
Shippensburg, PA 17257-0310

"Speaking to the Purposes of God for This Generation and for the Generations to Come."

**For a complete list of our titles,
visit us at www.destinyimage.com.**